ALL OVER THE WOLD

By the same author

THE BEVIN BOY

ALL OVER THE WOLD

DAVID DAY

SEVEN BOWES-LYON

First published in 1998 by
SEVEN BOWES-LYON
Moreton-in-Marsh
Glos. GL56 0EN
Tel: 01608 651622

Copyright 1998 © David Day

ISBN 0 9532454 0 3

Printed by Ebenezer Baylis & Son Ltd
The Trinity Press, Worcester and London

Contents

Author's Note — vi
Illustrations — vii

Chapters

1 Pre-Cotswold — 1
2 Moreton-in-Marsh — 18
3 Places — 31
4 Heigh For Cotswold! — 44
5 Royal Visits — 58
6 Centenarians, Etc — 63
7 Shakespeare — 69
8 The Law — 75
9 Estates — 82
10 Play-acting — 87
11 Parish Councils — 94
12 Obituaries — 99
13 Linage — 105
14 The Smiths Move Out — 111
15 Capital Of The Cotswolds — 126
16 The Giants Move In — 143
Index — 153

Author's Note

THIS BOOK TELLS of my experiences as a newspaper reporter in the Cotswolds from 1948 to 1984. It is not a guide to the area though it mentions many of the sights that visitors come to the Cotswolds to see nor is it a history though it touches on the past when this concerns events of the present. Abler reporters may feel that insufficient space has been given to the more aggressive type of journalism. All I can say is that this aspect of my work existed but nothing seems to date faster than yesterday's controversy: the humorous and offbeat stories last longer. I would like to thank the Editor of the Evesham Journal, the weekly newspaper by which I was employed, for allowing the use of a number of pictures taken by the staff photographers who were my colleagues: also the people of the North Cotswolds, to whom this book is dedicated, for their forbearance during the years that I was privileged to be the chronicler of their activities.

Illustrations

William Garne and his "Cotswolds" 1966 (Ch 4)

The Pasque flower 1956 (Ch 4)

The old trout, Blockley 1955 (Ch 3)

In Chipping Norton's fire-gutted town hall 1950

The Queen, Queen Mother, Duke of Edinburgh and Prince Charles at the Central Flying School, Little Rissington 1974 (Ch 5)

The Queen, accompanied by Commandant Harry Judge, meets firemen after opening the Fire Service College, Moreton-in-Marsh, 1974 (Ch 5)

At the opening of the Cotswold Farm Park 1971

At the Four Shires Stone with motor cycle 1949 (Ch 2)

Mr. Harvey with Nip and Spot, Moreton-in-Marsh 1950 (Ch 4)

Pier Paolo Pasolini directs "The Canterbury Tales" at Chipping Campden 1971 (Ch 10)

As pall bearer, ringing a bell, in "The Pardoner's Tale" 1971 (Ch 10)

Stow's oldest resident, Mr. Harrison, plants a tree on Coronation Day 1953 (Ch 4)

"Is this my father?" The two Mr. Capers, Aston Subedge 1953 (Ch 6)

Burnt Norton bicentenary with Viscount Sandon R in period wig 1953 (Ch 9)

Capt. Spencer-Churchill, seated third from L, with his tenant farmers, Northwick Park 1956 (Ch 9) Photo: Eric George

As Father Christmas at the Playhouse, Moreton-in-Marsh 1965 (Ch 10)

North Cotswold young farmers in their prize-winning nativity play, mid 1960s (Ch 10)

CHAPTER ONE

Pre-Cotswold

FROM THE TOP of the ladder, high up in the trees, I could see the Cotswold ridge only a few miles away, crowned by that quaint architectural chesspiece, Broadway Tower, where the hills reach one of their highest points, just over a thousand feet above the sea. On leaving school at the end of July, I had no idea what career to follow and till the examination results came through I was plum picking in the orchards of the Vale of Evesham, the Worcestershire town where I was born and grew up. The vale is sheltered to the east by the Cotswolds and to the south by their outlier, Bredon Hill, and you are aware of the nearby protective hills wherever you go in and around Evesham, an old town enclosed within a loop of the drowsy River Avon. When I was a small boy going to church and heard the preacher talk about lifting up your eyes unto the hills, I took it for granted that it was the Cotswolds to which he was referring.

The plum harvest was almost over when the School Certificate results appeared in mid-August and my future, after returning my ladder to the orchard foreman, was still undecided. I had passed in all the subjects I had taken, news that both pleased and dismayed my father, who had been so persuaded that I would pass in nothing that he had obtained a dispensation from the county education authority to remove me from the grammar school while I was still under sixteen. (I had taken the examination early at the age of fifteen.) He had been so discouraged by the adverse end-of-term reports on my progress that he could see no point in throwing good money after what he considered to be bad on my education. I tried explaining that it was the marks on the reports that mattered, not the teacher's uncomplimentary comments, but he was convinced that I would be better off at work, earning my keep, and my mother, who had died the previous summer, would no doubt have agreed with him had she lived. She had regarded it as an extravagance to send me to the grammar school in the first place.

My father, who was in his mid-fifties, had been in charge of the drapery department of one of the larger stores in the High Street for over thirty years. He and my mother moved to Evesham in the quiet years before the First World War, not long after their marriage, when there were still more horses to be seen in the street than cars and when farm carts and drays would rumble into town on market days. When I called at the shop to inform of the examination results, he offered to buy me a watch, presumably to atone for his previous lack of faith in my abilities, but I unforgivingly declined his gift. As it happened, I was going to cost the poor man considerably more than the price of a watch during the months ahead.

On visiting the school to collect my certificate, I was shown into the presence of the headmaster, who asked what I was doing or proposed to do. I explained I had not got a job yet apart from plum picking, which was now over, and after taking a look at the certificate and noting that I had achieved "distinctions" in English Grammar and English Literature, he said "Well, English is obviously your strong subject. What about trying to get a job with the local newspaper?" The idea of becoming a reporter had not occurred to me until then, no-one in the family, past or present, having been connected with journalism, and it sounded far more interesting than the job my father had in mind. He had arranged for me to be interviewed at the Inland Revenue office, where I was being offered employment as a junior clerk, a position that he regarded as of enviable promise and stability. I did not share his enthusiasm but had so far failed to respond with an alternative, nor could I prevaricate much longer.

On the way back from the school I called at the office of the local weekly newspaper, the Evesham Journal and Four Shires Advertiser, and asked whether they could give me a job. I was taken upstairs to the editorial department and introduced to the Editor, Reginald Monnington, who struck me as being one of the most genial men I had ever met. It happened that he and my father were cronies, the two of them having served together with a local ex-Servicemen's association, he as treasurer and my father as secretary, and this obviously worked to my advantage. It also happened that I could not have called at a more opportune time. The paper's most active young reporter - indeed, its only active full-time reporter - was about to be called up into the Forces at Christmas and it was high time that they started training someone to succeed him.

It was now the late summer of 1942, the Second World War was about to enter its fourth year, and as each young man reached the age eighteen, he was conscripted for military service. This meant that a school leaver had no more than a year or two to get established before being whisked off to war and that businesses had to cope with an endless turnover of younger employees. No sooner had one been trained and made a useful than another had to be found to replace him. The Evesham Journal had already got through several young reporters since the war began and when I came away from the office that day, I had been invited to be the latest in the succession, starting the following Monday.

Despite my headmaster's comments, I doubt whether I was chosen because I had been to a grammar school and done well in English in the School Certificate examination. On the contrary, they usually chose a boy from the elementary school who had left at fourteen with no bits of paper in his pocket at all. What they were looking for was someone who sprang from the local community and had a liking and enthusiasm for the people and the district. They wanted a person prepared to efface himself and become blotting paper to absorb what he heard and saw, then put it down in writing quickly, accurately, impartially – and anonymously. It was the paper that spoke, not an individual. The idea of employing a reporter desirous of holding the centre of the stage himself would have horrified them. Bylines were unheard of.

I was eager to accept the job but first I had to win over my father. He was not averse to my choice of career and liked the idea of my working for Mr. Monnington: the stumbling block was my wages. The Journal were offering me five shillings a week, or twenty - five pence in today's decimal currency, a dismal wage even for those days of low pay. They promised that after a month's probation I would be given fifty pence but this was small comfort to my father, who was himself on modest wages, out of which he would have to go on subsidising me as substantially as if I had remained at school. It was , perhaps, because he still had a twinge of conscience about removing me from school prematurely, that he gave his consent to my becoming a reporter, low wages and all, and I started work, as arranged, the next Monday.

The Evesham Journal and Four Shires Advertiser, circulating in the counties of Worcestershire, Warwickshire, Gloucestershire and

Pre-Cotswold

Oxfordshire, came out each Friday and sold 24,000 copies. It had an incomparable circulation area, consisting of the Vale of Evesham with its sprout fields and asparagus beds; Pershore, circled white by plum orchards in the Spring; Bredon Hill, with its coloured county views over the Severn and Malvern hills beyond; Tewkesbury, mothered by its ample abbey church and chequered with half-timbered houses; Stratford-upon-Avon and the South Warwickshire villages, with their legends and mementos of Shakespeare, and the Cotswold upland where, as a result of the war, some of the smaller villages in their snug valleys had reverted to the self-sufficient way of life they had enjoyed for centuries after the rich wool trade declined, leaving the district by-passed and forgotten. Its revival as a tourist magnet had yet to come.

The area was thick with history. Major battles had been fought at Evesham, Stow-on-the-Wold and Edgehill, and apart from Tewkesbury Abbey, monastic remnants survived at Evesham, Pershore, Hailes, Winchcombe and Deerhurst. Cottages were of timber and thatch in the vale and honey brown stone on the hills, and vivid stately homes rose over such places as Ragley, Sudeley, Compton Wynyates, Coughton, Charlecote, Stanway, Sezincote, Batsford and Chastleton. Older than any of these were the Rollright Stones, a prehistoric stone circle, near Chipping Norton, and Belas Knap a mysterious long barrow above Winchcombe.

It was an area to stir the heart of a fledgling reporter!

When I started work that Monday there were three important things to be learnt. The first was to type, and this was achieved by giving me a machine on which to hammer away in a corner till I had taught myself. Within a day or two I had become adept as a two finger typist and gradually built up a speed which may not have resulted in total accuracy but which served my reporting needs adequately, then and after. The second was to write shorthand, which proved far less easy to do. Despite what some advertisements say shorthand takes a great deal of time to master and for a person like myself, learning it in his spare time, it was obviously going to take anything up to two years of practice before I had built up an acceptable speed. As I did not have this sort of time, I was obliged to make do with my longhand – fortunately, I had always been a fast writer – and work in shorthand symbols as and when I acquired them. The result was, I regret, a bastard shorthand that would have shocked the purist and done me little good if I had been obliged to produce my notebook as evidence in court but at least it made me take extra care about accuracy. Within a year I was to be called on to undertake just about every assignment in the reporting calendar and I could not wait for my shorthand to catch up. I enrolled for evening classes at the grammar school, which I had so recently left, and had private tuition from a middle-aged maiden lady who led me into the perplexing world of "shun" hooks and grammalogues and dictated practice pieces about the breeding habits of rabbits, but my shorthand progress was slow.

The third, and possibly the most important skill to be learnt was a news sense, though I am not sure whether this is something that can be taught: you either have it or you don't. Later on, I was often to despair of some of my friends who had first-rate news stories under their noses but failed to recognise them as such and inform me though they never failed to tell me about whist drives, weddings and similar mundane matters. Others seemed instinctively to know what news was all about. The man-bites-dog definition of the news is still valid though I am able to offer an authentic alternative, also involving a domestic pet. When a cat walked into a meeting of the Campden branch of the National Farmers' Union, which I attended, this was not news. When it proceeded to have kittens under the chairman's chair. which it did, this was news: in fact, it sabotaged the meeting!

My news sense was put to the test fairly soon. Among the humdrum jobs required of me was attending auctions to take note of the figures reached by properties on the market. I was sent to this particular auction at the Rose and Crown public house with instructions to do no more than record the opening and final bids: in other words, not to add embroidery of my own. The saleroom was curiously crowded with clergymen and when the last property, a piece of land in the Lenches, near Evesham, was offered for sale, they did something very unusual for men of the cloth: they did their best to disrupt the proceedings. They regarded the land as belonging to the church and not to the private vendor and made their views known by heckling the auctioneer, an action almost as embarrassing for them as it was for him. Eventually the sale had to be suspended and the property temporarily withdrawn. Despite my instructions I scribbled it all down, especially the bit when the auctioneer yelled, "This place is more like a C.of E. parrot house than a saleroom!" and when I got back to the office, typed out a report which was well received by the Editor and proved one of the major stories of the week. Happily, it looked as though I had passed my news sense test alright.

Among other humdrum jobs to be done was interviewing the water bailiff for our weekly angling column. As he was on one side of the Avon and I on the other, we had to shout to and fro across the river, he advising me, for example, that the water was "running very clear" or "in spate", the latter fact being fairly obvious because the current was almost swirling round my feet. I also had to call on the undertaker, a short, explosive man, who would stand in his white apron, ankle deep in wood shavings, finishing off a coffin,and berate the Journal for all the wrongs we were supposed to have done him. (It was usually because we failed to put the name of his firm on the end of an obituary report, a form of free advertisement for him). His censure extended not only to the management but to the lesser employees "with neither chick nor child" who, he complained, had none of his family responsibilities and led utterly selfish lives, and even to myself who, he said ought to be ashamed of working for such a contemptible firm, after my mother and father had brought me up so carefully. On cooling down, he would respond to the object of my visit by giving me the names of the latest departed and the addresses to go for the obituary report

I also had to call on the clergy and this could be tricky, too. The Roman Catholic priest would not reveal his forthcoming services, especially those on feast days, unless I had been to the Anglicans first because he suspected them of trying to copy his observances. He may have had some justification because the parish church was remarkably "High" in those days. Today, of course. ecumenism reigns.

It was a bleak and strange war-time world that we inhabited. Everything was rationed and there was a total black-out when night fell with not a light to be seen under the stars. The worst of the air raids was over but the sirens still sounded and you could see searchlights flashing and the glow of incendiary bombs to the north where the industrial areas lay. The town was ringed with military camps, drably painted or draped with camouflage netting to conceal their whereabouts, and the area swarmed with men in uniform, a growing number of them gum-chewing Americans, whose glamour tended to put our own boys in the shade. For the Journal to give the remotest hint that any of these camps existed was to invite prosecution and if any of the military came before the Magistrates, we could print no address or give any clue that they might be stationed locally; we could not even mention the state of the weather for fear this might prove useful to the Nazis. Members of the Home Guard, the civilian army, were likely to pop up from behind a tree or a bush and demand to see your identity card even though they knew perfectly well who you were. My father, who had been walking to the shop, morning and afternoon, for thirty years, was stopped by one of his friends in the Home Guard on his way to work and when he could not produce his identity card, was sent home to fetch it before being allowed to continue. A delivery of sausages, a rare commodity in those days, would send people stampeding to the shop in question to form an orderly, patient queue to be served, and it was no use going to he cinema after half -past seven at night because it was full.

Yet it was a wonderfully stimulating time in which to live. The country was determined to win the war and by now there was less doubt about what the result would be. Everyone had a cause, a contribution to make to the war effort, from old ladies knitting socks for soldiers to schoolboys gathering dandelion roots for making medicines. I was an A.R.P. messenger, which involved cycling between the various air raid warden posts after dark to keep them supplied with information from the control centre and rations from the Women's Voluntary Service at the Forces' canteen in the town hall. My rounds incidentally provided an excellent opportunity for news gathering at each of the posts I visited. At the Evesham Journal it was a source of pride that they had managed to bring out a paper, albeit in much reduced size, every week since the war started, despite the worst the U-boats could do to prevent the newsprint from reaching these shores and the German bombers, to frustrate the railways from delivering it to us. The staff, mainly men over conscription age or unfit for Military service, were dedicated to getting the paper out each week no matter how difficult the task might be.

The Evesham Journal was a typical family newspaper. Founded in 1860 by two brothers, William and Henry Smith, it was still being run by their kith and kin, eighty years on. As they all bore the surname Smith, we referred to them by their Christian names to avoid confusing them and us. Mr Raymond, son of Henry, was chairman of the board and occasionally lent a hand as a a reporter. He was often to be found in the boardroom preparing our "Looking Back" column, which reprinted items of news from twenty-five, fifty and seventy-five years ago. The heavily bound files of the newspaper, going back to the first issue, were kept there, as revered and treasured as the Crown Jewels. Mr Geoffrey, the managing director and grandson of William, was in charge of the paper's finances and Mr Kenneth, also a grandson of William, wrote the leading articles, which were of an unmistakable Liberal persuasion. This trio kept a benign eye on the employees, knowing each of them personally and making all the right noises when they thought you were doing well. Most of the staff had worked for the Journal all their lives.

The office was a modest red-brick building fronting on Swan Lane, a side street leading off the High Street. The ground floor accommodated the commercial and advertising staff with a private room for the managing director, while the first floor had a large editorial room with separate rooms at either end, one occupied by the boardroom and files and the other, by the Editor, who did all the subbing himself in those days. Behind the office lay a yard, then a far larger building, housing the printing works, which also consisted of two storeys, the upper floor being used by the compositors, who sat at their clattering machines, setting type for the week's news. At the centre was the flat, shiny "stone" on which the type was assembled and each page made up. One of my tasks was taking copy across the yard to the comps room and as I appeared through the door I would be met with a chorus of catcalls and whistles, an experience that turned my face scarlet at that age. They were only joking – no doubt to relieve the monotony of their tedious, sedentary job – yet in my experience there was always a touch of hostility in the attitude of the printers, who saw themselves as the key workers of the paper and regarded reporters as having a cushy time compared with them. The truth is that a good paper depends on the efforts of the reporters to get the news and the advertising people to attract the revenue. The printers have nothing to do with the stature of a paper. They can stop publication, of course, but this is an entirely different matter. The ground floor was the home of the huge printing presses that caused the building to tremble on Thursday afternoon when we went to press and they were put into motion. These nether regions were the haunt of the ink-stained, overalled machine men, who were surlier than the comps above and I was glad not to have to enter this part of the premises often and run their scowling gauntlet.

Thus, the whole Evesham Journal set-up, advertising, finance, editorial, type-setting and printing, was all contained within a single, compact site, and this contributed to the close-knit, family atmosphere almost as much as having the original Smiths still at the helm.

Soon after Christmas the young man, whom I had been appointed to replace, went into the Navy, having reached the age of eighteen, and I took over the work that he had been doing, which included covering the magistrates' courts at Evesham, Pershore and Chipping Campden and the district councils at Evesham and Pershore. In common with many other similar authorities, the Evesham council met monthly round an open coal fire at the local workhouse, a proper Dickensian scene. In addition to me, the Journal had a veteran reporter, a man in his late fifties, who used to travel by bus or train from Alcester every day. He had no means of getting around other than on foot and could not take on evening assignments because he had returned home by then. Mr Raymond, also in his fifties, was available as a stand-by reporter and had a car, subject to the necessary petrol coupons being available, and we had full-time men at our Stratford-on-Avon and Tewkesbury branch offices, neither liable for call up, fortunately. We were a small team but by no means on our own. All over the area local correspondents were diligently sending reports, grammatical or otherwise, of happenings in their parishes, for which they were rewarded with traditional payment of a penny a line, and we were glad of all the help we could get.

The paper was an old-fashioned conventional broadsheet with its title in gothic lettering and its front page filled with classified advertisements or "smalls" as they were called. There was nothing stylish or imaginative about it and there were few pictures. The photo blocks had to be made in Birmingham, thirty two miles away. We sent off the pictures by bus and they returned by the same means a day or two later. We had a photographer, who had been a broken man since his only son, a very popular boy, had been killed in action with the R.A.F. and he now seemed resigned to a life of introspective semi-retirement. On those occasions when he emerged to work for us I treated him as gently as I could and perhaps because of this, it henceforth became a golden rule of mine always to be nice to the photographers who are a sensitive – you might almost say, touchy – breed, much given to returning from assignments complaining that the pictures they have taken are no good when in fact the reverse is the case. They are susceptible to digestive ailments, nervous problems and domestic difficulties due to the erratic hours they have to work and the pressure on them to get their pictures right first time. If a reporter botches a job he can at least camouflage the fact by making a couple of telephone calls afterwards. A photographer does not have a second chance as a rule. Upset, they become morose, discouraged and truculent. Handled diplomatically, they can work pictorial miracles.

I went everywhere by bicycle, bought from the proceeds of a previous season's plum picking. Going to Pershore was all right because it was only six miles away along a fairly flat road but Campden was three miles further and required a long haul up the Cotswold escarpment at Dover's Hill. I had the chance of taking lifts with Police superintendent Ernest Price, of Evesham, who prosecuted at Pershore, and with Henry Saunders, an Evesham solicitor, who drove to Campden, where he was clerk to the magistrates, but at the age of sixteen I was in such awe of these people that I preferred to rely on my bike, except when the weather was bad, despite the fact that both eminent drivers went out of their way to be affable when I was their passenger.

There was a silver-haired, elderly reporter at Pershore court, called Fred Crook, as upright as a skittle and fit as a fiddle, who had no hesitation in criticising the magistrates loudly if he felt they had imposed a wrong penalty. "Damned disgrace!" he would exclaim should a fine be too high in his opinion. "They ought to be ashamed of themselves! That man has a wife and four kids to support." The result was that when the magistrates announced their verdict, they would immediately swivel towards the Press bench to observe the reaction in that quarter!

The court cases consisted mainly of black-out offences, misuse of petrol coupons, contraventions of food rationing and failure to report for Home Guard duty. Pershore had a strong line in neighbours' disputes, which had led to blows and thence to counter charges of assault, while Campden sometimes yielded an application for an affiliation order in which a woman with child born out of wedlock would sue the putative father for maintenance. If he denied paternity, she would have to prove her case and I would listen with fascination as she described how, where and when copulation took place, sometimes completely losing the thread of my shorthand.

Although Campden, queen of Cotswold towns was only nine

miles from Evesham, I had never been there before, perhaps because the steep climb to reach it was a discouragement to cyclists from the vale. When I began covering the courts regularly, it was like going into another world; even the weather could be different up there. If it was foggy in the vale, as it often was during the winter, the skies would be clear and blue above Campden in its hollow in the hills, and to come cycling into that serene little town with its sparkling church tower and wondrous curving High street, hedged with rich Cotswold stone buildings, was to feel suddenly uplifted, and never more so than at that time when most of the outside world was tearing itself apart in a war.

The courts there usually went on into the afternoon, allowing me to explore the town during the lunch adjournment. Alas! There was nowhere to get a cup of tea and as I was still too young to go into a pub for a drink, I used to buy buns in a bakers' shop, then make my way up the tree-arched path to the church, where there was always a glass and carafe of water on a sill inside the porch. After eating the buns and drinking the water, I would wander inside the church and gaze up at a white marble wall bust of the lovely Penelope Noel, who died young in 1633, it was said from pricking her finger with a sewing needle, and stand beside the fifteenth century monumental brass of William Grevel, "Flower of wool merchants all" and one of the men who helped shape Campden when it was rich, busy and famous.

Often I did not get home until late evening. It had been obvious from the beginning that being a reporter would mean working irregular hours and that my leisure time would be invaded to the detriment of my relationship with other people. An unfortunate example of this occurred not long after I had joined the paper, when I managed to persuade a girl, whom I had long admired, to go to the pictures with me. A luck would have it, I was asked to cover a golden wedding at Dunnington, a village near Alcester, during the late afternoon of this particular day. It was about six miles away and I realised that I would have to hurry if I were to get back in time for my date, though I was sure that it could be done if I tried. In any case, I had been told to do this interview and had little choice about whether I went or not. This golden wedding stands out in my mind because the wife insisted that she and her husband had not had a cross word in fifty years; then when I asked him where he was born and he replied, "Here", she turned on him angrily, saying, "You daft old fool!

Pre-Cotswold

You wasn't born here, you was born at Wixford!" and a good old set-to took place, leaving me wondering whether she had misled me or whether I had been the cause of the first rift in their fifty years of married bliss. The interview lasted longer than anticipated and I had powerful head winds against me all the way back, which slowed me down badly. It also started to rain, and when I got to the cinema, half-an-hour late, the bird had not unexpectedly flown. Even now I feel a shiver of embarrassment at the thought of that lovely creature being kept waiting outside Hampton's sweet shop, opposite the cinema, and she never agreed to out with me again. Nor do I blame her. Newspapermen are not punctual boy friends or spouses.

A melancholy aspect of my work at this time was calling on the relatives of Servicemen, who had been killed in action: the parents of sons who had died, or young wives who had lost their husbands. Of course, there was sometimes good news, a gallantry medal won or person presumed dead, now found alive in a prisoner-of-war camp, but mostly the news was bad, very bad. I used to feel like a wheeled Angel of Doom, cycling about the town or villages in pursuit of the pathetically brief details of the latest war victim's short life. Often they were boys whom I had known, who had been in a form two above me at school. When I rode into a street, people would recognise me as the Journal reporter and watch and see which house I went to, curious to know which family had received the latest fateful message from the War Office. There was scarcely a home without someone on active services about whom bad news could be received at any time.

When I visited bereaved families there were rarely any tears. All they wanted to do was talk. I was invited in, offered a chair, asked whether I had known the dead boy, told what a wonderful person he had been, given his letters to read and taken up to his room to see his belongings. The family photo album was brought out, I was shown the things he had made and souvenirs he had brought home on his leaves. If anything, the mothers and wives seemed glad of the chance to open their hearts to someone outside the family, and I was often the first such person to call. I learnt a lot about bereaved people then. Later in life, I would get irritated with over-protective relatives, who wanted to keep me away from a husband or wife who had lost a partner; in the majority of cases, I found the survivors glad of the opportunity to talk to me, both for the satisfaction of discussing someone who had meant a great deal to them and to ensure that the dead person's worth was adequately recorded in the paper's obituary column. As for myself I always felt that if people had been good enough to take the Journal all their lives, the least we could do was to see that they got a decent write-up when they died.

Yet I must confess that there was another side to these war-time visits about which I ought to have felt ashamed but rarely did. As I listened sympathetically to what the relatives were saying I would, at the same time be looking round the room to see whether there was a photo of the dead person to borrow for the paper. While expressing regret over his loss, I would be thinking that the picture on the mantelpiece of the boy in his uniform would make a very good single column block and on hearing, for example, that he had twice narrowly escaped death, the headline, "Third Time Unlucky", would flash across my mind. The more interesting his previous exploits were, the more I would scribble it down in my note book, congratulating myself on having come across such useful copy. A part of me was cold-blooded, and in this respect I showed no reform as I got older. I suppose that every reporter must suffer from this awful dichotomy of feeling compassion as a human being for the plight of another individual yet at the same time being unable to deny his excitement at discovering a good story, recognising the victim's lamentations as excellent "quotes" and visualising the whole yarn as it would appear on the page, with photos if possible, in the next issue of the paper. It is a Jekyll-and-Hyde condition endemic to the business, I fear.

That my two years with the Journal in Evesham were so rewarding was largely due to the Editor, Mr Monnington, who proved as genial to work with as he had been when I first met him, on calling at the office for a job. Then nearing fifty, he was tallish with curly iron-grey hair and a full face with patrician nose and old pipe, sticking out of the corner of his mouth. As with Shakespeare's Falstaff, whom he much resembled, he was ample to the fore but carried himself well with a hint of a swagger, enhanced by the dashing angle of the wide-brimmed trilby hat he wore. Like Falstaff, he loved to hold court and spin yarns containing a fair measure of boasting especially where his prowess as an Army Officer in the First World War was concerned. Indeed, he could be a bit of an old ham. When I used to poke my head round his office door, he would bury his face in his hands and moan, "The very worst has occurred!" or roll his eyes upwards and exclaim, "Oh, Lord! What have I done to deserve this!" Every so often during the day we would hear his firm steps along the corridor and the door of the reporters' room would burst open as he came in to regale us with more of his stories. He had a ribald, irresistible sense of humour and , as far as I could tell not a whiff of bad temper in him. He was always very kind to me: I think that he had a soft spot for all junior reporters, who probably provided him with his most impressionable and receptive audience. Towards the end of the afternoon, he would enlist my aid in doing "The Times" crossword puzzle, describing it as the best general knowledge test that anyone could have . He also had his share of Falstaff's timidity, disliking confrontation or any kind of unpleasantness. If an irate reader were reported to be on his way upstairs he would rapidly disappear into his sanctum, leaving us to fend off the invader if we could; and like Falstaff, he enjoyed imbibing at the local hostelry, the Star, where he had a pint or two of ale every lunchtime and came back to the office, refreshed and full of information he had heard. He was one of the best news gatherers I have ever known.

What I did not appreciate until I was older, was that he was also a first -class newspaperman, setting high editorial standards for himself and expecting the rest of us to do the same. He insisted not only on our getting the facts right but stating them as concisely as possible, one of his favourite expressions being, "Boil it down!" He would repeat this over and over again if he felt I was being too prolix at the typewriter, stressing the point by hammering me over the head, schoolmaster-like, with a rolled copy of the nearest newspaper to hand. If a report were critical of an individual or institution, he would require us to give the party concerned an opportunity to comment on it before publication, and if a request were made for a report to be suppressed, he would certainly ignore it and see that this particular report appeared if nothing else did. With his encyclopedic knowledge, he could spot a solecism a mile off, and he was a good district man, caring as much for the outlying villages as he did for the town, where the bulk of our sales were. He gave us all standards to work by and this made life so much easier for us as our careers developed. We knew exactly what our rights and responsibilities were.

Another person of whom I saw a great deal was my rival, Les Phillips, of the Evesham Standard and West Midland Observer, which belonged to the dreaded Berrow's Newspapers, of Worcester. They owned many papers in the West Midlands and had a habit, so their critics said, of buying up the opposition as and when they could. The Standard had been in existence for almost as long as the Journal and had a better situated office than we did, in High Street, but its circulation had never been a patch on ours.

When I joined the Journal I was warned about Les and told to have nothing to do with him, which was rather pointless because I was bound to meet him at most of the "diary" jobs we covered. In fact, he and I were thrown into each other's company so often that it was inevitable we become friends, at the risk of annoying our editors, who regarded such inter-paper fraternisation with suspicion. It is anomaly of journalism that reporters who would almost cut each other's throats in pursuit of a story, invariably get on well, drinking together, swopping jokes and putting on a united front when they feel collectively threatened or slighted. I always got on well with all the reporters I met from other papers and became more friendly with many of them than I did with my own Journal colleagues, of whom I saw less and less in the course of my own work after I moved to the Cotswolds.

Although he was the same age as me, Les had left school at fourteen and was thus two years' ahead of me in experience. We were both tall but otherwise dissimilar, he having bushy dark hair and a pale skin, I thick red hair and a pink complexion. He relished his notoriety with the Journal and missed no opportunity to enhance it. He would literally rub his hands together with glee when I informed him of the latest allegation of his "villainy" to reach our ears, he having almost certainly invented it himself. He seemed to enjoy being thought of as a rascal though the opposite was true, and he was a good deal more vulnerable and soft-hearted than he was prepared to admit. As he was unwelcome at the Journal, I would visit him at the Standard office where the current issue would be carefully opened to reveal a news story that we had not got. If I failed to react, he would point to the page with his finger and say "What do you think of that, then?" to which I would respond by producing a copy of the Journal from my pocket and drawing attention to a story that he had missed. He would reply "I knew all about that but it wasn't worth bothering with", and I would say of his story, "I wouldn't have touched that with a bargepole," and thus the banter would go on till we tired of extolling the virtues of one paper to the detriment of the other, and decided to push back the furniture in order to practice our dance steps, provided the Standard editor was out and not expected back soon.

Both of us wanted to become better acquainted with the opposite sex and the recognised way of doing this at that time was to go to one of the multitude of dances held in the local village halls every weekend. As we could not compete with the mature, uniformed glamour of the Servicemen, especially the Americans, we hoped at least to impress our partners with our ballroom skill. We sought private tuition from an Evesham dance instructress and enjoyed the weekly thrill of clasping her around the waist while she elegantly and impersonally led us through routines of three basic dances, the slow waltz, quickstep and foxtrot. On Friday or Saturday evening, all spruced up, we would cycle to places like Honeybourne or Fladbury to spend a night of music and potential romance in their village halls, where the floors were as slippery as an ice rink due to the excess of pre-dance rosin put down. A saxophonist, double bass player, pianist and drummer would sweat out the tunes from the stage while overhead, in the centre of the ceiling, a multi-faceted silver ball, without which no dance would be complete, quietly rotated, flashing light patterns round the room. Cycling home afterwards, we would discuss the charms of our various dancing partners and the success of our reverse turns, while bombers throbbed overhead, nightingales sang in the glades and glow worms in the hedgerow defied the black-out.

By the summer of 1944 the district had become emptier and quieter than at any time since the war began. The military, who had crowded everywhere, had vanished, almost overnight, and were now engaged in the D-Day invasion of Europe, a mission for which they had been training and waiting for so long. I, too, was getting ready to go. In the Spring of that year I reached the age of seventeen-and-a-half and registered with my age group, after which I was required to attend a medical examination along with many other young men, in a requisitioned Nonconformist chapel in Worcester. I could not help wondering what the elders of the congregation would have thought of all those naked men parading round their holy-of-holies, yielding up urine samples and coughing to oblige the doctors, who grasped the appropriate appendages! I passed A1 and was interviewed by a recruiting officer who put my name down for the Army.

Just as my predecessor had trained me to succeed him, so as my eighteenth birthday approached and conscription loomed, another school leaver was engaged for me to train to take over my work at the

Journal. It was rather like knocking the nails in your own coffin. Then, only a few weeks before my birthday, I received a shattering letter from the Ministry of Labour and National Service, telling me that I was not to go in the Army after all. My number had been drawn out of a hat and I was to be sent into the coal mines instead, compulsory service in mining having been introduced the previous year as an alternative to serving with the Armed Forces.

My father started to draw up an appeal, using such phrases in respect of myself as "being of an artistic nature" and "totally unsuited for manual work", but I could see there were no genuine grounds for appeal. If I were healthy enough to serve in the Army , there was nothing to prevent me from going into the mines. Mr Monnington, who had a streak of Welsh radicalism in him, was delighted at the prospect of my going to live in a mining community. "What a wonderful opportunity!" he said. "Make the most of it, laddie!" Les Phillips just laughed and said, "Coal output is sure to go down!" A fortnight after my birthday I received another letter telling me to report to an address in a coal mining area the following Monday to be trained for working underground, and for the next three years I languished as the inhabitant of a melancholy region where slag heaps rose like mountains and where I spent most of the day far away from the sunlight. At night I often dreamt of Campden.

CHAPTER TWO

Moreton-in-Marsh

WHEN I WAS released from coal mining and came back to the Journal after the war, all the jobs at Evesham had been taken by ex-Servicemen, whose demobilisation had come earlier than mine. The situation was aggravated by stop-gap reporters like myself, who had been taken on during the war, returning in addition to the original pre-war staff and there might have been a crisis over my future had not our man at Moreton-in-Marsh, a former Army captain, decided to resign and move elsewhere after eighteen months in the job. Mr. Monnington welcomed me home by telling me that I was to take over as the Journal's new reporter in charge of the Cotswolds and after three years and three months down a coal mine it was like being directed into paradise.

Moreton had been chosen as the location of the Journal's Cotswold branch office because it was the centre of local government for the area. The North Cotswold District Council had their offices in High Street and the town was well-placed for a man to get to Stow-on-the-Wold, Bourton-on-the-Water, Blockley and Chipping Campden, the four chief places to be covered in addition to Moreton itself. There was also a fast and frequent train service from Oxford to Worcester, which called at Moreton station, enabling copy to be sent to Evesham quickly and easily. I was given large printed news envelopes to use for my copy and supplied with rail stamps of interest to collectors, who would call at the office to ask whether I had any of the used stamps to spare.

My instructions from head office were clear. I was to live in the Cotswolds and become involved in the life of the community and not attempt to commute the fifteen miles between my home in Evesham and Moreton every day. I was to cover the various courts and council meetings and generally report on the activities of the district, favouring no particular place but reflecting the life of the area as a whole. I was especially asked not to keep ringing up the Editor and asking him what to do. I was to make my own decisions. As long as I kept the Cotswold copy coming through I would hear nothing from him nor would he expect to hear from me except to be told when an envelope had to be collected from the train at Evesham. In other words, I was to be my own boss, working on my own for the first time, and I moved to Moreton on the first Monday in January, 1948, four months after my twenty-first birthday.

The Journal was as parsimonious over office accommodation as it was over wages and I found myself housed in a dark, damp back room behind a shoe shop and boot repairers' in a side street, next to the Congregational church and opposite the Working Mens Club. The office was approached down a flagstone passage with Wellington boots of various sizes littering either side and sheets of leather hanging from the walls, and was heated by a paraffin stove, which kept it comfortably if odorously warm but was liable to send a flame shooting several feet into the air if mishandled. The proprietor of the premises was Percy Lloyd, who was born in the neighbouring village of Longborough and had spent all of his life locally apart from his service in the Machine Gun Corps during the First World War. He and his wife, both nearing fifty, took me under their wing from the start, inviting me into their domestic quarters behind the shop to ply me not only with tea or coffee but also with any news to have come their way. The office would have been left untended for hours while I went on jobs had they not stood in for me, answering the telephone and taking messages. They were virtually unpaid assistants.

The building was double-fronted and must have been handsome at one time. Built of Cotswold stone during the 18th century, it still displayed elegant Georgian details despite having been converted into shops. A girl looked after a shoe shop on one side while Mrs Lloyd ran a tobacco and sweet merchant's on the other. Mr Lloyd and his men did the repairs in a workshop up the yard while upstairs, over my office, was a bookmaker's, which was operated discreetly by telephone, this being before the days when betting shops were accessible to the public; and newspapers, magazines and toys were also sold from the premises. With such a profusion of commercial activity going on, there was a risk that my shy office might be overlooked and so a panel bearing the paper's title in the inevitable gothic lettering, was displayed on the wall outside.

Another more effective inducement for people to come into the office existed. The Evesham Journal was the major advertising medium of the North Cotswolds and the recorder of local births, marriages and deaths, and in addition to reporting duties I was required to take advertisements, a task repugnant to any journalist worthy of the name but a responsibility that I was unable to refuse. I got no extra money for doing this job, which could be both irritating and time-consuming, yet I must confess that the advertising was a draw and brought many more people into the office from all over the district than I would otherwise have seen, an advantage to me at that stage. The more who came in, the more I could ask about what was going on. As a newcomer in unknown territory I needed all the eyes and ears I could get.

It was an extensive territory too. There was well over a hundred square miles of high Cotswold to be looked after, nearly a third of the Journal's total area, and I was obviously not going to be able to do it by bicycle. I tried for the first three weeks but was defeated by the steep, interminable hills, not to mention the robust winds. As I was in no position to buy a car, still a luxury for the majority of the population, the firm provided me with a motor cycle, a mode of transport previously unknown to me. The first time I took out the machine it led me straight into a hedge, the beginning of a thoroughly uncomfortable partnership that was to last seven years. I even managed to fail my driving test, no mean feat bearing in mind I was completely out of the examiner's vision for most of the time. He passed me after the second test, inquiring, "Are you using the machine for business or pleasure?" When I told him it was for business, he drily replied, "It didn't look as though there was much pleasure about it!"

It was not just that I kept falling off. I often could not start the machine. I used to wonder whether the designer of the motor cycle had suppressed homicidal tendencies because among the components to be adjusted before starting were the ominously named clutch, throttle and a strangler. The machine certainly induced murderous feelings in me, especially if I missed the kick starter and gashed my shin in consequence. At the first kick the motor might splutter but show no sign of bursting into life. At the second kick, the same thing would occur and at the third, fourth, fifth, and sixth, by which time there would still be no life and now no splutter. This would call for some spanner work. After removing the sparking plug to see whether the gap was damp or bridged by a metal whisker, I would work the kick starter up and down several times to remove any "richness" that might have gathered inside the cylinder, then replace the plug and try the kick starter again. Of course, the motor would remain as dead as ever.

There was only one thing to do then. After lifting the valve compressor, I would put the engine into gear and run the motor cycle along the road, preferably in a downhill direction, and as the pace quickened I would close the compressor and the engine unless completely done for, would roar into action. Racing alongside the wakened animal I would take a jump and land, with any luck, across the saddle and facing the direction in which the machine was going. Admittedly, there was certain exhilaration to be gained from speeding up hill and down valley in the fresh air but tomorrow the machine would have to be started all over again and I could never be sure how it would respond. One night, in a fit of temper, after finding I had left a critical spanner behind, I threw all the other tools over a hedge before starting the long push home, after the motor cycle had broken down. The next morning, on calming down, I had the embarrassment of returning to the spot and retrieving the tools from where they had fallen among the dew-damp thistles and cow parsley.

After a motor cycle journey during the winter I would enter meetings looking like Father Christmas with a windblown, rubicund face and frost whitening my eye brows and hair. During the summer there was an insect hazard with midges in my hair and wasps up the inside of my sleeve to sting my arm. I devised a means of appearing at social functions looking reasonably smart, whether it was pouring with rain or snowing, by wrapping myself in a cocoon of oilskins. The problem was finding somewhere safe and inconspicuous to stow my gear when I arrived. On visiting stately homes, of which there were many in the Cotswolds, I would abandon both machine and outer clothing halfway up the drive and walk the rest of the way, hoping that when he opened the door, the butler would think that I had just left my car round the corner.

Three years after the war, it was still a bleak world in which we lived, with most commodities rationed, including the petrol for my motor cycle. I used to lie in bed in the early morning in my "digs" and listen to the Germans and Italians tramping to the railway station at dawn on the first stage of their repatriation from the Cotswold prisoner of war camps, where they had been working on the land for several years. Some prisoners chose to stay, married local girls and became naturalised Britons enriching the electoral role with their tongue-twisting foreign surnames. Coming the other way were harassed refugees, such as Poles, Lithuanians and Estonians, who moved into the camps that the prisoners had vacated at Northwick Park and Springhill, where the huts survive to this day. Only the camp at Bourton-on-the-Hill was cleared and the site planted with healing conifers.

Austerity ruled. Among the meetings I had to cover were those of the Food Control Committee and the Fuel Economy Committee, the purpose of which was to see that rationed supplies were fairly distributed and not wasted. It rankled with people of the Cotswolds, who suffered from severe winters, that their coal ration was less than that for the snug Vale of Evesham, just because the latter was marginally further north on the map and in a differently fuel zone. When an officer of the Ministry of Fuel and Power appeared at Campden Magistrates' Court to prosecute an individual for alleged misuse of fuel, he had the tables turned on him by the Bench who, in announcing their verdict, complained about the unfairness of the coal allocation. They said the Cotswolds had been the coldest place in Britain during the previous winter yet Worcestershire, which most people would regard as more sheltered, was allowed more coal per household. The officer won his case but left the court with his tail between his legs yet despite this and other protests, no adjustment took place though the Ministry conceded that applications for extra fuel from the elderly and invalids would be "sympathetically" considered.

Perhaps the most vivid example of how we lived then is provided by my first report from the Cotswolds, which stated, under the heading, "Parcel From The Princess":

> "Here's a parcel for you from Buckingham Palace," said the postman to Mrs. Beatrice Olive Hudson, of Longborough, on Thursday, when to her surprise she was the recipient of one of the food parcels sent from abroad as a wedding gift to Princess Elizabeth.
> "The parcel, which contained fourteen tin of various fruit and vegetables, was accompanied by a letter in the Princess's own handwriting which said: "Many kind friends have sent me gifts of food at the time of my wedding. I want to distribute it as widely as I can and share my good fortune with others. I, therefore, ask you to accept this parcel with my best wishes."

It is unlikely that a member of the Royal Family would be flattered to receive tins of food today yet they were highly acceptable to everyone in those days whatever his or her station.

A preoccupation at the time was preparing for a Third World War, which was expected at any moment now that an Iron Curtain had fallen across Europe and the Soviet Union was behaving so suspiciously. The North Cotswolds had a full-time Civil Defence Chief and there were uniformed volunteers all over the district who regularly held training exercises, the biggest of which, Operation Oakleaf, took place in 1954 and involved not only the Civil Defence but the Fire Brigade, Ambulance Service, Police, the lot. The scenario was that an atom bomb had dropped on Birminghan and that its victims were pouring into the district, as indeed they were in the form of numerous non-local folk impersonating refugees, many dripping with blood, while one poor soul had nothing but clothes she stood up in and her pet canary in a cage. To make matters worse, several high explosive bombs, alias thunderflashes and smoke candles, fell on the hapless village of Broadwell, while incendiaries, in the guise of magnesium flares, rained down on Bourton-on-the-Water. Despite all this the emergency services managed to cope and by nightfall all the injured had been treated either in hospital or on the spot, and billets found for the homeless.

These exercises always provided an excuse for a good deal of emergency cooking on makeshift outdoor ovens and the Civil Defence Corps achieved its masterpiece in 1955 when it cooked an alfresco stew consisting of 2cwt of potatoes, half cwt of carrots, 75lbs of beef, 28lbs of onions and 10lbs of flour and proceeded to feed it to more refugees, impersonated by American Servicemen, who must have dearly wished they were back on the Normandy beaches again! Happily, the next World War never came and the perils of the atomic bomb and emergency cooking mercifully receded.

The Cotswolds are not so much a range of hills as an undulating plateau, rising imperceptibly from the east, near Oxford, and falling dramatically about thirty miles to the west to form a tree-dotted escarpment overlooking the vales of Avon and Severn. The best of Cotswold is in Gloucestershire though some edges into Oxfordshire and the new county of Avon to the south, and its characteristics are a pattern of stone boundary walls, isolated dome-shaped clumps of beech trees, shimmering green in spring, aflame in autumn, and warm-coloured villages of a distinctive, much copied architecture, all mullion windows and steep, moss-flecked stone slate roofs. The beauty of the Cotswolds is unusual because it results very largely from man's achievement. The contours of the landscape and its colouring are nature's but human hands have fashioned the network of fields and boundary walls and built the stone villages, which grow from the earth as if they were part of it. Other regions have loftier hills and broader valleys but in them man has frequently been an intruder. In the Cotswolds, as nowhere else, he and nature have worked harmoniously together.

The usual image of the region is of a street of handsome stone houses and a Perpendicular church rising beyond, paid for from the proceeds of the profitable medieval wool trade, but this is not the complete picture. Despite their seclusion, the Cotswolds have as long and continuous a history of habitation as any in the country. Bourton-on-the-Water and Stow-on-the-Wold stand either on or adjacent to the earthworks of prehistoric camps, and the Roman-built Fosse Way bisects the area from north to south, providing a legacy of Imperial remains on either side of the route. Farmers turn up flint arrowheads and ancient coins with their ploughs and the foundations of old abandoned villages going back to Saxon times, have been discovered. A more accurate picture of the Cotswolds would be of a knot of stone cottages in a valley by a trout stream with a Norman church, containing Saxon work, a Roman villa hidden somewhere in the woods, and an ancient burial mound on the hill.

For several centuries sheep rearing was the great trade of the Cotswolds. Wool from the old Cotswold breed was long and soft and much in demand during the late Middle Ages and Tudor times, not only in this country but abroad. Italian importing merchants knew the Cotswold town of Northleach, one of the great English wool centres, as Norleccio, for example. The hills were like a vast sheep run, reflected in the glamorous fifteenth century churches and other buildings constructed during this prosperous period. Then, the wool trade went into decline and during the eighteenth and nineteenth centuries the Cotswolds became a forgotten backwater, a tragic demotion for their inhabitants, who still had their bread to earn, though it undoubtedly resulted in the area surviving unspoilt into the twentieth century, a sleeping beauty to be awakened by the kiss of modern tourism.

Immediately after the Second World War, though, there were few tourists about. The streets of the towns and villages had more of a green leaves and grass than chrome and metal; parking problems were unheard of and many traders still went their rounds on horse-drawn vehicles. Some of the tranquillity of the old days briefly lingered on.

I rang the police and fire brigade each morning to see whether crime or catastrophe had occurred and started to do a weekly round of the district, calling on such informed people as parsons and postmistresses, though this was not a success and had to be dropped after a while. Some of the parsons got tired of seeing me: one refused to receive me at all, saying that I was not really interested in his church, only in learning through him of other people's misfortunes. The remaining parsons kept feeding me with bland items about confirmations and Sunday school prize-givings, which I found unexciting, thus no doubt vindicating the worst suspicions of the parson who refused to co-operate. The postmistresses enjoyed seeing me and would go on talking for hours but I came to realise that they were getting more information from me than I was from them, and the little they gave me was trivia when, as I later discovered, other more newsworthy events had been happening within their orbit.

I turned my attention instead to building up contacts in each of the forty odd towns and villages, whom I could telephone regularly, or who better still, would ring me, transfer charging the call, if necessary, when they heard of something interesting. Our chain of village correspondents had been crumbling since the war and few were left in the Cotswolds. Many had regarded their contribution to us during the war as a form of local patriotism, no longer relevant, or considered the reward of a penny a line as insufficient for cajoling information from their neighbours or turning out on a cold evening to cover a meeting. I tried to keep the surviving few happy by calling on them occasionally and making them feel we were interested and grateful but as far as the bulk of the Cotswold copy went, it was obvious that I would have to be the provider, assisted more by contacts than correspondents. The exception was sports reporting. With so many different matches being played on a Saturday afternoon, I could not hope to get to more than one and so we depended on club secretaries to send in reports. I had a go at covering home football matches at Moreton but had difficulty in identifying the scorers and had to run alongside the linesman after each goal to discover from him who they were. This distracted him, provoked the spectators and embarrassed me, and led to my having to delegate the reporting of matches at Moreton, too. Cricket match reports were written from borrowed score books, where the numbers of runs scored rarely added up correctly, making it necessary to juggle with the "extras" till the total came out right.

After three sterile years as a square peg in a round hole, in the coal mines, I was enjoying my new life and already feeling that this was where I was meant to be and where I wanted to stay. A temporary handicap was that I still looked and felt too young for the role I had to play as sole resident journalist in the North Cotswolds. An early assignment was to accompany a party of students from the Royal Agricultural College to Snowshill Hill, a showplace farm, whose wealthy owner, John Bourne, wearing a brown trilby and a white smock, showed the lads round with me trailing behind, notebook in hand like the rest of them. As I had no idea for most of the time what esoteric farming process Mr Bourne was describing, I had to keep tugging the sleeve of his farm manager for elucidation. It did not take the man long to work out that this particular student, who could not tell the difference between a grain drier and an automatic bagging machine, knew nothing about farming even though he might look no different from the rest of the college party. At last he felt obliged to seek elucidation, too, and demanded, "You are an agricultural student, aren't you?" "No" I replied, relieved that the truth was coming out, "I'm a reporter."

I also tended to be awkward with the big fish I had to interview, though they swam in only a small Cotswold pond, and was irritated to find myself reddening and stammering when I most wanted to appear self-assured. I dreaded dinners, which most reporters regard as one of the perks of the job, a free night out with plenty to eat and drink. The trouble was that you found yourself in a room full of pigeon fanciers, footballers, beekeepers or members of some other fraternity with whom you had nothing in common and maintaining a conversation with your neighbours at table for two hours could be an ordeal for someone as tongue-tied as me. At a Conservative dinner at Campden, a stately gentleman next to me, dismissing my youth, said "Sir, by your presence this evening, I take it that you are of the same political persuasion as myself: therefore, allow me to introduce myself," and gave me his name. I gave him mine without revealing why I was really there though the reason became all too apparent when the dinner was over and I had to draw out my notebook and pencil to take down the speeches, another disadvantage of dinners. After amply wining and dining, you felt more like going to sleep than having to report what the after-dinner speakers had to say.

As it happened, my "persuasion" was not at all similar to the gentleman's at that time. Some of the miners' radicalism had rubbed off on me and when a meeting was called in Campden to promote the Labour Party I decided to attend and give them a write-up. That such a meeting was to be held in an ultra-Conservative town was almost news in itself. To stand up and be counted as a Labour supporter in a Conservative stronghold requires strong convictions (and presumably vice-versa in a Labour stronghold) with the result that the minority meetings of the Left in the Cotswolds, though dismally attended, usually had more impact than the more populous gatherings of the Right. At General Elections, when the Labour candidate had not a ghost of a chance of winning, the faithful, gathering in a near empty hall, would sit themselves round his table for an intimate man-to-man discussion that oozed comradeship and integrity.

This Campden meeting was presided over by Tom Benfield, a working man with grizzled hair and strong hands, the chairman of the town's tenacious Labour branch who, in his opening remarks, was much exercised about the shortcomings of the Board of Guardians, who ran the Workhouse and whose title he insisted on pronouncing to rhyme with "sardines". The principal speaker was a Labour evangelist from outside the district whose pep talk I reported at length and sent off to Evesham where the Editor, to my surprise, printed it in full under a conspicuous headline. I can only imagine that they were short of copy that week! The result, which I ought to have foreseen, was that the Conservatives then insisted on inviting me to their meetings, expecting the same kind of expansive treatment, and after this I found it prudent to avoid political meetings as much as possible.

Over twenty years later, the trustees of the Campden Almshouses, one of the great architectural set-pieces of the Cotswolds, a graceful stone terrace, sheltering under the tall, chiming church tower, modernised the buildings and suggested I interview the tenants to see how they felt about the improvements and include their comments in my report. One of the tenants proved to be Mr. Benfield, now a dignified old man, who showed me around his home, praising the work that had been done. As I was leaving, he said "I remember you! You came to one of our Labour meetings once and gave us the biggest write-up we ever had. I shall never forget it – seeing our meeting splashed all over the paper like that. It was the biggest boost to our morale we ever had." Nothing in my career gave me a greater pleasure than that this veteran political warrior should have remembered me with gratitude after all those years.

The Journal did not like Party politics and I was discouraged from attending the monthly Press conferences given by the local M.P., whose constituency included Cirencester and Tewkesbury as well as the North Cotswolds. All four constituencies in the Journal's area were safe Conservative seats and political activities were inevitably one-sided. To have reported all of them would have meant giving more space to one Party than to the other and appearing biased, which the Journal was not. It was a truly independent paper; and so politics usually took a back seat in our columns between General Elections and when these took place, strict rules were observed. Each candidate had his picture and potted biography published; his adoption meeting was reported and one – but only one – of his pre-Election meetings, and everyone got the same amount of space, even if it meant getting out a ruler to measure it. As a weekly paper we also completed our Election reporting in sufficient time for a candidate to be able to reply before the polls to any damaging allegation against him that we might have reported the previous week.

Not that anything as controversial as this ever happened. Elections in the Cotswolds were invariably polite and dull, all except the 1950 Election, that is, when the district had its first and last Communist candidate and a very unusual one at that: the Eton educated, the Hon. Wogan Phillips, later to become Lord Milford, whose political views belied his upper class station. While the other candidates played to half-empty halls, his meetings drew the multitude, there half out of curiosity and half out of a desire to heckle him. Many of Mr. Phillips' own background came, apparently regarding him as some kind of traitor to their class, and their heckling was abusive and puerile: you half expected them to resort to the language of the Remove and cry, "Oh! You rotter, you! You absolute cad!" But Mr. Phillips handled them with dignity.

There was a memorable exchange when a working chap. Danny

Wasson, a good Roman Catholic if ever there was one, rose at Moreton and demanded of the speaker, "Do you believe in God?"

"I am an atheist," Mr. Phillips replied.

Danny rose again his face red with anger and his close-cropped silver hair bristling. "That's not answering my question!" he shouted. "Do you believe in God?"

The Conservatives won the election as usual, of course.

Few notable politicians came into the area. The Prime Minister, Clement Attlee, visited Moreton with his wife in September, 1950, but this was only to have tea at the White Hart while his car was filled up with petrol. His visit coincided with the heaviest thunderstorm of the year and flooding occurred in the High Street due to blocked drains. Harold Macmillan addressed a Conservative rally in a marquee at Sudeley Castle, Winchcombe, in June 1954 when he was Minister of Housing and the Premiership still lay ahead. I had his silky tones directed at me briefly when he paused in his speech and asked, "Would you mind resting your pencil a moment?" while he said something off the record to his audience.

At a dinner of the Campden branch of the National Farmers' Union at the Lygon Arms, Broadway, one of the handsomest hotels in the kingdom, the guest speaker was Gerald Nabarro, an M.P. famous for his large moustache and the loud voice with which he used to ask questions in the House of Commons about purchase tax, a subject on which he was an expert. His talk to the farmers showed him equally knowledgeable about agriculture. Immediately after the speech-making, I made for the exit, as was my wont, only to hear footsteps following me down the corridor and I turned to face Mr. Nabarro, who had come after me with a sheaf of papers in his hand.

"I believe you are from the Press," he said. "Would it help you to have a copy of my speech?"

I thanked him and said that it would, whereupon he handed over the papers, adding "I have marked a particular passage which you might care to send to the Press Association and make yourself a bob or two." (It is not unusual for a local reporter with an interesting story to try it out on Fleet Street in addition to supplying his own paper. If it is used, he gets paid for it.)

The passage was something about calling on the Government to act at once to save British Agriculture and I told him I would phone it through as soon as I got back to the office.

"Why not now?" he said. "you'll catch the early editions then."

I told him I didn't know what the number of the Press Association was though I had it back at the office.

"I have it here," he replied suavely producing a notebook from his pocket. "We can use the telephone kiosk in the hotel. It won't take more than a couple of minutes."

The two of us then squeezed into the kiosk with Mr. Nabarro instructing me on which number to dial, the procedure to follow on getting through and how best to put over my copy. I felt I was in the hands of a real professional.

The exercise over, we squeezed out again, he thanked me for co-operating and I thanked him again, and we went our separate ways, I to my motor cycle in the hotel yard and he, back to the dining room to rejoin his farmer hosts.

Neither of us profited from the exercise. That evening the Queen announced the engagement of Princess Margaret to Anthony Armstrong-Jones, a sensation that dominated the following day's papers, almost to the exclusion of everything else. It was certainly not a morning for hard-hitting facts about British Agriculture!

CHAPTER THREE

Places

EACH OF THE five small towns or large villages, whichever you prefer, that I had to cover, was completely different from the others. They were all roughly the same size, just under or over 2,000 in population when I moved to the Cotswolds. Moreton was the most extrovert, being at the intersection of two main roads, the Fosse Way from north to south, and Oxford to Worcester road, from east to west, and it had a main line railway station from which there were frequent trains to and from London. The town was easy to get into and out of and there was nothing unusual in seeing strangers in transit, breaking their journey for refreshments at a café or hotel. The inhabitants were not in the least isolated or clannish by disposition except in the sense that certain families predominated, almost all with surnames beginning with an aspirate: the Hoopers, the Hardimans, the Howes, the Hathaways and the Hornes. One resident, Mrs. Harvey Haine, excelled herself in having a surname with a double aspirate.

A mile up the road stood an ornamental pillar, known as the Four Shires Stone, where the counties of Worcester, Warwick, Oxford and Gloucester met until 1933 when an island of Worcestershire was transferred to Gloucestershire, since when only three counties join there. It has been said that Moreton got its name because it was situated near these boundaries or marches – in other words, that it was Moreton-in-the-March but this is now rejected. The town's name means exactly what it says. Moreton lies in a flat area under the hills on a wet site, liable to flooding though, "marsh" would be an exaggeration today after all the drainage schemes put in hand there. At one time the town was called Moreton Henmarsh, which explains why the name developed into "in-marsh" and not "in-the-marsh".

There was something about Moreton that reminded me, not too seriously, of a Wild West town: the broad, straight main street with buildings on either side labelled "Bank", "Hotel", "Blacksmith" and "Undertaker", and raised pavements or sidewalks and an old horse trough still in situ. It was the sort of setting where you could imagine a pair of gunmen plodding towards each other at dawn for a final shoot-out, and the railway station stood close by on a line running straight as an arrow for miles across flat country towards Adlestrop, like the railway does in the wide open spaces of the West. No Western town, though, had such a green avenue of tall lime trees to relieve the emptiness of its main street or such a solid and conspicuous town hall, bang in the middle of the road. The hall was built in the late nineteenth century by Algernon Bertram Freeman-Mitford, subsequently the 1st Baron Redesdale, who lived at Batsford Park, Moreton's great house, and was grandfather to the Mitford girls, Nancy, Unity and the rest, whose early years were spent there after their father succeeded to the title.

The hall was built in stone to resemble a Tudor market hall with open arches, where people waited for buses or sheltered from the rain. Above was a cathedral-like assembly room with high-timbered roof, stained glass armorial bearings in the windows and utterly inadequate heating. Nor was heating the only problem. It was my painful task after each Magistrates' court to report that a number of male citizens attending dances in the hall had been fined for urinating in the street because the lavatories inside the building were so inadequate. At last, the owner, the 1st Baron Dulverton, who acquired both Batsford Park and the town hall from Lord Redesdale, donated his "white elephant" to the district council who promptly destroyed the character of the hall by filling in the ground floor arches to accommodate better lavatories though this action undoubtedly rescued the male population from further acts of indecency and ignominy in the columns of the Evesham Journal.

Of the big five North Cotswold parishes, Moreton was the least regarded for its architecture and beauty, having too much red brick and blue Welsh roofing slate to qualify as pure Cotswold. Its church was uninspired Victorian and apart from the Redesdale Hall there was nothing remarkable to catch the eye, yet the appearance of the town was by no means unattractive; its buildings, though ordinary, blended nicely together and the High Street curved attractively on its western side. Moreton was something of a philistine among the Cotswold towns, having little cultural activity, not even a dramatic society, an essential everywhere else. What it lacked in culture, however, it made up for in sport with capital football and cricket clubs. The great W.G. Grace played on Moreton's beautiful cricket ground and county matches were revived there with success after the war.

    Blockley was the opposite of Moreton in almost every way. Not only was it bursting with cultural groups but it had a sumptuous setting to put Moreton's flat surroundings to shame. It was a village of stone terraces ensconced deep in a comely valley, whose slopes mingled open pastures with plentiful woodland, and there was a touch of theatre about the way the houses, church, chapel and so on posed at different levels, one overlooking the other on the valley's side: a kind of jack-in-the-box architecture where one minute you would be looking down on a building and the next minute, looking up at it. There was a greater sense of seclusion in Blockley than in any of the other big five parishes, partly because there was no through road of importance. It was easy to by-pass the village and this was how the inhabitants liked it. Offers from publishers to include Blockley in their guide books were rejected and well-meant attempts by the district council to promote tourism in the village were resisted. Though as pretty as anywhere in the Cotswolds, Blockley did not want to become a tourist attraction, which was probably just as well because every road in and out of the village involved negotiating a steep, dangerous hill. The only time I got benighted as a Cotswold reporter was after attending an evening meeting in Blockley when an unexpected snowfall silted up the roads and defeated all my efforts to drive home up the hill.

    The numerous springs on the slopes above Blockley were a major source of the North Cotswold piped water supply and also fed a stream that descended through the village, pausing every so often to replenish a quiet pool, now merely ornamental but once the provider of power for the several silk mills that briefly made Blockley an industrial village during the nineteenth century. These mills had long since been converted into desirable residences, complete with rippling water gardens, whose reflected light flickered on the ceilings of the rooms inside. It was a pool in a garden that took me to Blockley in April, 1955, in a week when guns sounded at the Tower of London to mark the Sovereign's Birthday, the flag of St George flew in honour of our patron saint and diplomats walked to Holy Trinity church at Stratford-on-Avon to do homage to the Bard on the anniversary of his birth. My visit also had to do with an anniversary though no guns sounded in Blockley, no flags flew or diplomats walked, yet exactly one hundred years before died he whose fame spread all over the world and whose grave was regularly visited by curious pilgrims. He did no great deeds nor did he change the world for the better or the worse. It is not even recorded that he had a name. All that we know of him comes from the epitaph inscribed on a tombstone that stood in the cottage garden.

> Under the soil
> The Old Fish do lie;
> 20 years he lived
> And then did die.
> He was so tame,
> You understand,
> He would come and
> Eat out of your our hand.
> Died April the 20th
> 1855. Aged 20 years.

Since his death the Old Fish, a trout, had been widely written of in newspapers and magazines and it seemed appropriate that I should give him some form of eulogy when his centenary came along in 1955. What I had not bargained for was that the tradition he began lived on in that same pool, where during his short life-time he swam into the shoals of fame. Another trout, perhaps a lineal descendant, occupied those hallowed water when I called and he, too, was so tame. you understand, that he would come and eat out our hand. Unlike the Old Fish, however, his successor had the advantage of an Evesham Journal photographer to record for posterity his propensity for hand-feeding. Thus, the glory that was, survived into the present age to be captured on film.

The arts flourished because Blockley had an attraction for academics, who made it their week-end home, and they and other notables, including a trustee of the National Gallery, a former Governor of the B.B.C., an eminent botanist and several well-known water colourists, were able to lure interesting people to speak or perform in the village. Blockley had the best hall in the North Cotswolds, built during the war of masonry from an estate lodge hit by a German bomb, and I was present at its opening, having cycled up from Evesham in my apprentice days to report the proceedings. The only blot on the village's reputation was that for a number of years it had more suicides than all the rest of the district put together. The chosen means of despatch were rarely the same and the victims came from all social groups, natives as well as outsiders, the poor as well as the comfortably off. The epidemic, if that is the right word for it, stopped as suddenly as it had started and the village resumed the normal ways of mortality, but attending a succession of Blockley inquests as a young man left me wondering whether suicide is entirely the result of anxiety and depression or whether there is a contagious element about it, too.

Blockley claimed to have been the first village in England to have electric light. A powerful lamp, put on the church tower in 1887, was said to have cast a glow like moonlight over the streets, the presence of water power having made the experiment possible. Something similar happened each Christmas when an illuminated Christmas tree was hoisted up the side of the tower to be erected at the summit, not so much to spread the Christmas message across the valley as to keep the tree safe from vandalism.

At Bourton-on-the-Water they put their Christmas tree in the middle of the river for the same protective reason and very pretty it looked at night with its lights reflected in the water. The Windrush, still no more than a stream, flows through the centre of the village, giving Bourton its name, to which hyperbolists have added the additional title of "Venice of the Cotswolds" without a great deal of justification. In the old days Bourton looked far more pastoral than it does now. It always had charming stone houses, several of architectural distinction, but the Windrush was just an ordinary brook wandering through an ordinary meadow, which also happened to be a village green. Then in the early years of this century, this informal heart of the village was smartened up; the meadow became lawns, the river was neatly channelled between Cotswold stone embankments, and elegant little bridges were thrown across it to give Bourton that Venetian look. The village became too charming for its own good; visitors began to jostle in and when "Bo" Morris, the landlord of the quirkily-named Old New Inn, built a Cotswold stone model village in his back garden, this soon became famous and established Bourton as the most popular of all Cotswold villages. It was there, I am told, that I took my first steps as a child, tottering after the ducks on the river while on an afternoon outing from Evesham with my parents.

As petrol came off the ration and car ownership spread, crowds poured into Bourton on summer week-ends and the village became a target for charabanc parties of the middle aged and elderly from all over the Midlands. As the traffic grew, so did the commercialisation, and not just the usual cafés and gift shops. At various times the village boasted a witchcraft exhibition, an aquarium, a model railway, an aviary and a motor museum, in addition to the model village. Alone among the North Cotswold big five, Bourton had an overcrowding problem, the scene on a fine Bank Holiday being almost absurd. So many trippers would have packed themselves on to the village green that there was scarcely a blade of grass to be seen. Indeed, there were times when the village was literally full up with queues of traffic waiting to come in and the police pleading with the drivers to go back home. Yet many of the visitors knew the odds, having been to Bourton before, and came again because they genuinely liked the place, crowded or not. The irony was that when they were not there, during the winter or in the early morning, Bourton looked as pretty as it had ever done. The visitors unwittingly spoilt the very thing they came to see.

The popularity of Bourton gave the village elders many a headache. They were opposed to garish advertising and admonished traders who offended in this respect. The commercialisation of Bourton has been deplored but, personally, I found its appearance far more tasteful than that of some of the holiday villages in the West Country and Lake District. There was also a problem of too many feet wearing out the village green, which had to be re-turfed or re-seeded at intervals or, more drastically, fenced off for a season to give the grass a chance to recover. Then there was all the litter to be picked up. The parish workman, a cheerful Irishman named Paddy Kenneally, worked like a Trojan but occasionally lost his cool and instead of removing the litter, would deposit the entire week-end's haul in an enormous pyramid on the village green in an attempt to shock or shame the public into being tidier. The chief perpetrators had all gone home by the then but it helped him to let off steam and the height of the heap was a salutary reminder of just how much litter got left behind.

Because Bourton was so popular, any charity event held on the village green could be relied on to raise a considerable sum, due to the many visitors; and the parish council, the custodians of the green, had to impose a rigorous booking system. If there were more than one applicant for a "goldmine" date such as August Bank Holiday, a draw was made at a council meeting, and I once had the honour of being asked to rest my pencil and perform this task. I drew Bourton Roman Catholic church from the hat for which I hope they were truly grateful when the takings from their annual fête began to roll in.

Another more unusual problem was the noise made by brass bands, causing Councillor Norman Galloway to tell the council in 1962 that he would like to see the number of bands on the village green curtailed. "We get more like Blackpool every day," he said. "We get enough noise from the trippers and their cars without having to put up with brass bands. They are a real nuisance to the people living in the centre of the village. Some of the bands play quietly but others go all out on their trumpets."

The parish clerk, Tony Davies, warned that more bands were wanting to play in Bourton than ever before.

Councillor John Taylor said, "A resident who complained to me, suggested that once a month was not unreasonable but Sunday after Sunday was a bit too much."

Councillor Ben Woolley added, "If I was living near the village green I know that I would object," but Councillor Amy Donovan replied there were worse things than brass bands.

"They are on to a winner, going round with their collecting boxes with the hundreds of people we have visiting the village," Councillor Galloway said. "It's a real money-spinner and we are the sufferers. There are enough attractions here for trippers without having brass bands. I would like to see the number of bands limited to four a year, and when the green is let, the band should be asked play… What's the word?"

Councillor Joe Steward: "Pianissimo!"

The council decided to restrict the number of brass bands visiting the village to once a month during the summer and ask them to play pianissimo, and this remedy must have worked because no one complained about the bands again.

As at Blockley, there were many newcomers living in Bourton, usually retired and well-to-do, and in both places they meshed harmoniously with the natives; never more so than at the annual flower show, when the population of both villages was at one in its enthusiasm for the event. It was a pity, perhaps, that Campden did not have a flower show to induce this unifying effect because the tension there between "them", namely the newcomers, and "us", the locals, was never far below the surface.

The native Campdonian had an intense local patriotism. He revelled in recalling events that happened long before the newcomers arrived, thus demonstrating his impeccable Campden pedigree, and in talking about characters that only someone who had spent all his life in the town could possibly remember. A comparative newcomer who asked a true-blue Campdonian how long it would be before he was accepted, was told that it would not be until he could produce a father and grandfather who had been born in the town. For their part, the newcomers, many of exceptional knowledge and experience, felt they had an obligation to do their best to protect the beautiful town in which they had chosen to live. They might not be indigenous but they knew an eyesore when they saw one and were determined to resist any development that might spoil Campden as so many other old towns had been. The natives, always ready to do battle, regarded this as presumptuous and interfering. The newcomers, while wishing to antagonise no-one, argued that Campden was far too precious for them to stand idly by while harmful changes took place.

An example of this sort of confrontation between the natives, speaking for Campden people, and the newcomers, for Campden town, ran all through the nineteen-fifties when the locals wanted to have electric street lights in the High Street and did not care whether this meant concrete monstrosities as long as pedestrians could find their way safely after dark. The situation was aggravated when a popular character, called Wally Stanley, was knocked down by a car and killed while crossing the street after dark, and inadequate lighting was blamed for the accident. The newcomers felt that the existing Victorian lamp standards were more appropriate to Campden and opposed the change, and year after year they were in the majority at the annual parish meeting at which the subject was debated. When the original standards became so dilapidated as to be dangerous, the town replaced them by buying secondhand gas standards from Birmingham, where they were less squeamish about going over to electricity, and very fine pieces of Victoriana they proved to be when re-erected in Campden's streets. Despite this, the pro-electricity faction persisted and eventually won, their vote being decisive, of course. Having chosen to go over to electricity, the town could hardly go back to the old gas standards the following year after uprooting and scrapping them all. Even so, good taste prevailed. The newcomers maintained that Campden deserved something special and the

Electricity Board, which had been hoping to unload stock concrete standards on the town, was persuaded to provide graceful bronze metal columns and lanterns instead, and these were much admired and copied by other places.

These perennial "them-and-us" clashes were, of course, meat and drink to a reporter like myself. At a town council meeting it was pointed out that a local lorry driver, Frank Nobes, was continuing to park his vehicle in The Square overnight despite being asked not to do so because it looked unsightly. As he was present at the meeting, as an onlooker, Mr Nobes was asked by the Mayor, Councillor Leslie Brodie, whether he had anything to say by way of explanation.

"I don't see why a working chap can't put a lorry in his own Square, Les," Mr. Nobes replied. "Why should I be kicked out just to please outsiders?"

The Mayor remarked that there were other places where the lorry could be left. "You are being very obstinate, Frank," he said, "and I can't understand why. You seem to have got it into your head that there is something personal about this but we have got nothing against you as an individual at all."

"The working class are behind me," retorted Mr. Nobes.

"It's only the nobs who are against me."

The council decided to take no further action for the time being and eventually Mr. Nobes yielded to the nobs and shifted his lorry elsewhere.

Another meeting rejected a proposal that the houses in High Street be numbered. "I knows where you lives and you knows where I lives," Ernie Buckland told the Mayor. "What does it matter about outsiders?"

The liveliest culture clash took place when a Campden body, known as the Robert Dover's Games Society, asked to re-erect a mock wishing well in the High Street which had raised a large sum for charity the previous summer. The arbiters of taste, the newcomers, were dead against it, of course.

Jack Nelson, a headmaster, who had retired to Campden, told a public meeting, "We have one of the finest High Streets in the country and the important thing is that all the buildings are genuine. This wishing well is entirely out of keeping with Campden. Some say it is all right because it makes money but there are appalling ways of making money. It is said that last year the wishing well was the most photographed object in Campden, and if so I think this is a great pity.

I am sure the Robert Dover's Games Society could find some other way of raising money and that this blemish on the fair face of Campden need not be put up again."

With a Scots name and accent to go with it, Seumas Stewart was obviously no Campdonian but was chosen to reply because he was a lively speaker and also vice-chairman of the Dover's Games Society, which otherwise consisted mainly of what you might call local blokes. "Those who made this well," he said, "did so from their hearts and in the best way they knew. Had it been made in the same way with the same materials one-hundred-and-fifty-years ago or more and devoted to the same purpose, it might now be treasured as a piece of folk art, and the people who seek to have it removed would say, "Let us keep the well!" but it is not antique, it is something new and so they say, "Take it away!" Last year two thousand people or more approved of the wishing well by voting for it with their pockets, and if the well is not re-erected I shall hang a pair of voluminous bloomers, half mast on my television aerial, to mourn the loss of honest to goodness human vulgarity in our midst by those of high artistic sensibility who have forgotten what it is to be human."

Once again good taste prevailed. The majority decided against the wishing well, which was not seen again, and Mr. Stewart was left to hoist his bloomers on his television aerial if he so wished.

The last of the five big parishes, Stow-on-the-Wold, shunned the security of the valley and sat on top of a hill, giving rise to the saying, "Stow-on-the-Wold, where the wind blows cold." The town was narrowly by-passed by the Roman Fosse Way and its huge Square, once a market place for sheep traders, stood deserted while the growing post-war traffic zoomed by, unaware of Stow's existence round the corner. The traders occasionally met to discuss how to attract these potential customers but failed to find a formula. Stow's Square remained a genteel backwater, where its finest domestic building, the 18th century St Edward's House, with a facade of fluted Corinthian pilasters, had a wire-netted poultry run on its flat roof in those days. Clucking hens would look down on the serene emptiness below: the spiky Victorian gothic of the town hall, the old stocks under the trees on the green and the numerous pubs. Only when the twice-yearly mops moved in did the town fill up with roundabouts, coconut shies and swings.

All Over the Wold

A stranger's first glimpse of the Square was all the more remarkable because the roads leading into it were so narrow, causing the spaciousness suddenly to burst on you unawares. Narrower still were the murky alleyways, known as "tewers", that provided secret short cuts all over the town. Eventually, of course, the traffic did penetrate the Square. Why it took so long is hard to say but Stow became, almost overnight, an "in" place, a "must" on the Cotswold circuit. The traders, who by this time were becoming top-heavy with antique dealers, rejoiced as the town bustled as it had not done for ages, though some of us pined for the quietude that had probably gone for ever. The Square overflowed with parked cars and going round, looking for an empty space, became a regular, fruitless ritual.

The population of Stow was less class-structured than that of the other Cotswold towns. In fact, you might describe them all as working people. There were the artisans, living on big council estates, like King George's Field; then the shopkeepers and tradesmen, and finally a sprinkling of professional people, like lawyers and accountants. There was no great house, no gentry and not all that many retired people. As a result there was little in the way of community tension, but not many flourishing organisations either, there being no influential figure to get things going. It is significant that the major Stow event in thirty years, the year-long celebrations in 1976 to mark the quincentenary of the completion of the Parish Church, was largely the inspiration of a vigorous Rector, Hilary Way.

Perhaps because of their contrary situation on top of a hill, the inhabitants of Stow had a stubborn, independent quality, symbolised by the Big Ben chimes of their church clock, which defiantly rang out of tune. Nothing made me feel more at home than hearing the cock-eyed chimes of Stow clock strike the hour! George Burden, the parish clerk at Stow, when I first began reporting there, was a typical example of Stow ebullience. A stocky, bald, fiery little man, he had scant respect for authority, an attitude shared by many of his fellow citizens. Of the district council, he said, "We don't want to go back to King Charles's days but the sort of thing they are doing is what he had his head chopped off for !"; of the county council, "It's about time we stopped being ruled by planning officers and the like and started to say what we want for a change. We have had enough of their physic!" and of the Government, "I think it's wrong to talk about Democracy when you don't have any say about whether you want to pay for things or not!" Short shrift was the only way to describe what he gave officialdom.

An example of Stow's reluctance to toe the line was their refusal to accept a new sewerage scheme, something that other towns and villages would have given a right arm for. On top of the hill, under the town, were deep cracks in the limestone strata, known as "swillies", and from time immemorial, drainage from the houses had been flushed into these, the inhabitants being well satisfied with this effective, cost-free natural amenity. The North Cotswold District Council was less enamoured of it and prepared a proper piped sewerage scheme, despite being opposed all the way by the town. The latter, realising that the council could not be stopped at local level, transferred their resistance to Whitehall, by lobbying the Minister of Health and M.P.s at the House of Commons, but no-one took any notice of them; the council's scheme was approved and implemented and drainage by swilly at Stow became a thing of the past. The saga was summed up in a poem I wrote for the Journal at the time.

In Stow-on-the-Wold from the dawn of creation,
The folk have disposed of their dish-wash this way:
By emptying it into strange holes known as "swillies"
Huge cracks in the rock, deep as coal mines, they say.

This system, which bountiful Nature provided,
The North Cotswold Council behold with dismay:
"You can't pour your swill in the ground," say the Council,
"Who knows where it gets to when it drains away?

"Stow climbed on its wold when the world was an infant
And there we desire it shall prosper and stay;
But under the Wold rise our springs and our brooklets,
Which dreaded pollution may strike any day."

"No" say the townsfolk, "this charge is unfounded:
Our spring are as clear as the mornings in May."
The Council decided a new scheme was needed,
For they have the Public Health Acts to obey.

As stubborn and proud as the hill that they live on,
The people of Stow told them, "Take it away!
This new-fangled scheme will waste ratepayers' money:
We'd rather use swillies, then no-one need pay."

A Stow deputation attended Westminster,
That Temple of Freedom, which all men survey;
They said, "Tell us straight, are we free to use swillies?"
The Government answered, emphatically, "Nay".

So Stow, which has boasted from time immemorial,
A system of drains costing nothing to lay,
Must now yield to progress, extravagant progress,
And empty its dish-wash the civilised way.

CHAPTER FOUR

Heigh For Cotswold!

EVERY FRIDAY AFTERNOON I would motor cycle to Evesham to collect my wages, hand in my week's advertising takings and obtain supplies for the office, mainly notebooks and copy paper. In the bad months of January and February I would stock up in advance in case I could not get through because of the weather. The Cotswold winters were harsh with deep snow drifts on the higher ground and the roads rutted with ice. Also reporting to Evesham were my colleagues from the other branch offices, Mike Ellis, from Stratford, Eric Simpson from Tewkesbury, and David Grant-Adamson, from Pershore, and after the obligatory appearance at head office we would adjourn to a café at which to swap our experiences of the week over a cup of tea, while outside the carillon of the venerable bell tower would tinkle tunes, like "Barbara Allen" and "The Bluebells of Scotland", over the roof tops. We of the branch offices were not altogether at ease at head office, where we did not feel we belonged and where the staff had a different outlook from ours. They may have even regarded us as a nuisance, a group of backwoodsmen descending on the office every week. Sometimes the four of us would talk about our futures. My own mind was firmly made up on this score. I liked the Cotswolds and wanted to stay there, a reaction no doubt intensified by those three years in coal mining, living in a district I disliked and doing a job at which I was no good. The other three went on to higher things. I alone remained.

I had obtained lodgings in Moreton with a retired farm worker, William Harvey, and his wife, Norris, both aged about sixty, who lived with their brown-and-white terrier dogs, Nip and Spot, at Ashbrook House, a gaunt residence in the nicest part of High Street, the quiet end, where the trees were taller and the grass verges wider and greener. Mr. Harvey had retired early because of heart trouble and was obviously not long for this world. He was a heavily-built man, which did not improve his condition, and had a brown walrus-type moustache, which made him look stern though he was the most good-natured of men. His wife was short and round, with her grey hair rolled into a bun at the back of her head, and was the warrior of the family, well able to stand up for herself should the need arise. As for myself, I was smothered with kindness by her, possibly because of an ordeal we had to share not long after I moved in.

Shortly before midnight I was wakened by an awful wailing coming from below and found Mrs. Harvey sobbing at the foot of the stairs, dressed in her nightgown with her hair undone and hanging lengthily down her back, giving her the look of a vulnerable schoolgirl. It was utterly unlike her to be seen in a dishevelled or emotional state and the reason was not hard to imagine. I went into the front sitting room, which had been adapted as their bedroom to avoid Mr. Harvey having to use the stairs, and saw him lying in bed, unmistakably dead with his face an eerie waxen colour. I helped Mrs. Harvey into the kitchen, where there were still a few embers warming the grate, then dressed and went out to a public telephone kiosk to ring the doctor, who had seen Mr. Harvey earlier that evening and who had fortunately not yet gone to bed. He said he was sorry about what had happened but had been expecting it and could see no point in coming round till the morning. I asked whether Mr. Harvey ought to be left as he was and the doctor agreed that something should be done before morning and gave me the name of a woman who, he had heard, was called in by families under such circumstances.

Although it was now nearer one than twelve, I visited this woman's house, which was in darkness, as all the houses were at that hour, and hammered on the door till someone, the woman's husband in his pyjamas, appeared at the bedroom window. I explained my predicament and without hesitation, his wife, who had now joined him at the window, also in her night attire, said she would follow me back to the house at once to perform the necessary ritual. With me on hand to help with the lifting, because Mr. Harvey was so heavy, she went about her task of laying out the dead man with a matter-of-fact competence that did much to improve my morale. Why she should have bothered to turn out in the middle of the night to oblige a complete stranger, I have no idea but she will always have my gratitude for doing so. With the laying-out over, I could turn my attention to Mrs. Harvey, who was now more in control of herself, and we spent the rest of the night, sitting in the kitchen, waiting for the morning to come. Soon after seven, I left to break the news to her brother, George, who lived nearby and who tried not to cry but could not prevent his eyes from watering. It was not until I saw his tears that Mr. Harvey's death became a reality. The night's proceedings had seemed more like a bad dream till then.

The Harveys had lived in a council house before inheriting Ashbrook House, which they had hoped to sell to give them something they had never had before: some money in the bank, but squatters moved in and the district council would only rehouse them if the couple moved into Ashbrook House instead. So, far from benefiting from their inheritance, Mr. and Mrs. Harvey had to give up their home in the village, where they had spent all their married life, and move into Moreton to occupy the cheerless Ashbrook House, which was far too big for them anyway. The squatters were a symptom of the times. Far and away the biggest problem of the Cotswolds was the shortage of houses, a deficiency that pricked the conscience of the community because many of the names on the long waiting list were those of Servicemen returning home from the war. The Housing Committee built as many houses as the Government would allow, even to the extent of putting up quickly-built but emphatically un-Cotswold Swedish timber houses and Cornish houses, made of pre-cast components, and the prefabricated bungalows erected during the war went on being used as homes far longer than their intended life span as the waiting list waxed rather than waned.

Another problem regularly aired was the lack of local employment. There were no factories in the North Cotswolds but this did not mean there were no industrial workers; on the contrary, there were a great many. It was estimated that at least a thousand workers travelled out of the district each day on over fifty buses to factories in the larger towns, and some people regarded this as a social evil that ought to be remedied by introducing light industry in the Cotswolds. I gave them all the publicity they wanted but was unconvinced by their arguments. It seemed to me that travelling to work resulted from improved transport and Cotswold men and women would have gone out of the district a hundred years ago had there been transport quick enough to take them to work and back each day. Nor, if local industry were provided, did it follow that workers would use it if they could earn more money, as they most likely could, by travelling away.

Farming remained the major industry, with corn and sheep on the wide uplands and dairy farming in the more sheltered pastures, and farmers formed the most influential body of Evesham Journal readers. I was invited to their National Farmers' Union branch meetings, which were a model of union democracy with the minutes of each meeting circulated to all members and branch resolutions forwarded to the county branch and if confirmed there, sent on to the London headquarters of the movement for implementation nationally. I used to call on a rota of farmers for their comments on such subjects as the crops, the weather and the harvest, and far from being unco-operative, they seemed delighted to be consulted.

I had to tread warily sometimes. One Easter, a number of telephone calls came through from upset naturalists, who had gone to see the Pasque flower at Kineton Thorns, a rough tract of grass, stones and scrub, five miles west of Stow, only to find that the area had been ploughed up. The Pasque flower, or anemone pulsatilla, is so called because it blooms at Easter, a gleam of purple amid the stony ground. Not only was there not a Pasque flower to be seen but another rare and prized inhabitant of Kineton Thorns, the Cotswold pennycress or thlaspi perfoliatum, had also disappeared under the plough.

I was taken to the site by a country lover and former horsewoman, now too arthritic to ride, who plotted our route by referring to various points at which she had come to grief in the hunting field: a five-barred gate, where she had broken her hip; a spinney, where her leg was fractured, and a field, where she dislocated her shoulder. It was an itinerary of past disasters as far as she was concerned. On reaching the site, I shared her and other naturalists' surprise that the land should have been ploughed. Littered with large stones, it looked an uninviting spot for cultivation, and I contacted the new owner, George Steele, a highly thought of farmer, to ask him why he had sent in the plough. He explained that the work had been done in consultation with the Agricultural Executive Committee and he and they were confident the land could be made good use of.

"I had no idea that botanists were interested in it or that rare plants grew there," he told me. "The land has been cleared and ploughed with the aid of a Government grant of £12 an acre for bringing land into cultivation which has been derelict. It has already been sown and should be producing crops for this year's harvest."

I decided that this was an occasion when neutrality was the best policy. I reported the facts absolutely straight and left it to the readers to decide which of the two crops they preferred: grain for the national larder or the anemone pulsatilla and thlaspi perfoliatum for the botanical handbook. Afterwards the ex-horsewoman telephoned me to say she was glad that I had not lambasted the farmer.

An interesting farming assignment was interviewing William Garne, owner of the last flock of the old Cotswold breed of sheep, at his home in the village of Aldsworth, near Northleach, when he was eighty-six, not long before he died. Over his mantelpiece hung an oil painting of sheep from the farm that won prizes at Canterbury over a hundred years before; the walls of the sitting room were covered with pictures of the family's champion sheep of yesteryear, all a heavy, rectangular shape, quite unlike the kind of sheep you see today.

Mr. Garne's sheep were the direct descendants of the mighty flocks that roamed the Cotswolds in the Middle Ages and gave the district its wealth, recalled by the "wool" churches and rich, stone architecture, and they lay in the same pastures they had grazed for centuries. For the Garnes had been on Cotswold for as long as the sheep had and they had always kept sheep. I asked Mr. Garne why he, alone among farmers, had retained the ancient breed. "I kept them on because of the name," he said. "We had always had them. I didn't think much about whether there was a future for them or not. All I knew was that I should go on keeping them for as long as I lived. What happened when I was gone would be up to my son. I have always liked sheep. They are not much trouble. We only bring them in for lambing, because they are better out. We don't even bring them in for lambing unless they start early."

I saw Mr. Garne at a time of a revival of interest in the Cotswold breed. Several new flocks had been started, all from his stock, and a Cotswold Sheep Society had been formed with, appropriately, Mr. Garne as its first president. The sheep were not as heavy as those in the old pictures but were still powerful, impressive-looking creatures with a heavy wool clip. When I jokingly asked Mr. Garne whether he thought the breed might one day restore the wealth of past centuries to the Cotswolds, he smiled and said, "No, I don't see anyone making vast sums of money from any kind of livestock any more. Of course, that's what built Northleach church – the Cotswolds, no doubt about that – and Cirencester church, too, but, then, you could build a church in those days for a fraction of what it would cost today."

An advantage of living at Moreton was that I was able to get up to London quickly and cheaply by train on my days off and was thus able to visit concerts and art exhibitions and see famous actors and actresses in their greatest roles. It was a case of having the best of both worlds: a life in the country and an easy access to the town. I was also able to visit the famous South Bank Exhibition during the Festival of Britain in 1951 and to wander the streets of London two years' later, admiring the decorations for the Coronation of Queen Elizabeth II.

The Festival of Britain was celebrated all over the Cotswolds, except at Stow, where it was felt that building materials were being wasted on frivolities on the South Bank when they should have been used for housing. Many places had qualms about whether post-war austerity Britain was the right time and place for a festival but went ahead with their plans and apart from the occasional hiccup, such as the judges' choice of a member of the Woman's Royal Air Force from Liverpool to be Moreton's carnival queen, to the consternation of the local girls, the year's events went off happily. General Lord Ismay, the chairman of the Festival Council, lived nearby and he and his wife attended several Cotswold functions, including the opening of four stone "Festival" cottages, built at the village of Stanton, only a few yards from the church in which the Ismays were married and within two miles of their home.

Coronation Day was, as far as I was concerned, a cold, wet marathon that lasted from half-past nine in the morning till after midnight. I spent most of the day on the saddle of my motor cycle, going round the towns and villages to record how they were celebrating the occasion, despite the wintry weather, and twice got soaked in the process. On my first round I left without putting on my gloves, a mistake that I did not repeat, and my hands were frozen after the first couple of miles. Each time I returned to the office to type up my reports, I went into the Lloyds' to get warm and catch up on the Coronation proceedings, which were being broadcast on their television set, before pressing on with my next round of calls. Television had arrived in the district at the end of 1949 and rapidly became popular despite much head-shaking over the effect that the aerials had on the hitherto unsullied Cotswold roof lines. The Coronation was the first great test of television and I was not the only person to drop into the Lloyds' to see how it was faring. Their sitting room was thronged with neighbours who had not yet got a set of their own.

One of the most popular ways of commemorating the Coronation was the planting of a tree but time proved that even this simplest of memorials had its hazards. Several trees died and Campden Woman's Institute's copper beech plain disappeared! Rumour had it that it was knocked down by a cow! Campden Royal British Legion also suffered a misfortune when they attended a grand review of ex-Servicemen in Hyde Park at which the salute was taken by the newly-crowned Queen. They mislaid their standard bearer, Fred Benfield, in the crush following the parade: a fruitless search was made for him and the coach on which he should have returned home with the rest of the party waited two hours before moving off without him. Mr. Benfield, carrying his standard, made his way to Marylebone Police Station, where he spent the night in the company of a large number of other ex-Servicemen, who had been similarly stranded. He got back to Campden safely by train the next morning, the Legion standard still in his hand.

The Festival of Britain and to a lesser extent, the Coronation, gave the district a fortunate legacy in the form of the permanent revival of the Cotswold Olympics, the great games founded by Robert Dover in the early seventeenth century on the hill that has since borne his name, above Campden. There were probably games on this site long before Dover, an attorney living at the foot of the hill, took a hand in them but from at least 1612 onwards they bore his name and were celebrated as the new Olympics in a collection of poems published in 1636. One contributor, Ben Jonson, felt unable to award the palm "twixt Cotswold and the Olympic exercise", while another, Michael Drayton, wrote of rustic merrymaking beneath a flag, inscribed "Heigh For Cotswold!", planted on top of the hill. Shakespeare also knew of the games and may have visited them himself "How does your fallow greyhound, Sir? I heard say he was outrun on Cotsall," says a character in "The Merry Wives Of Windsor". The Dover's Games, held each Whitsuntide for over two centuries, came to an end in 1851 after degenerating into rowdyism and looting: it was claimed that as many as 30,000 people were attending from all over the Midlands.

When Campden decided to revive the Games in 1951 it was to mark the centenary of the cessation of the games rather than to celebrate the Festival of Britain that same year though one good cause supported the other. A letter from Windsor Castle said the King had expressed interest in their plans and wished the organisers well, and the national newspapers were agog to learn that it was proposed to resurrect the ancient Cotswold sport of shin kicking for the occasion. In the old days, the competitors, wearing heavy boots, used to grasp each other by the shoulders and attempt to kick their opponents' legs in what was basically a test of endurance. As a form of training, they would have their shins clouted with a hammer or piece of wood and even treat their flesh to a form of pickling to toughen it up.

The revived Olympics were a tremendous success. The shin kickers were introduced with a touch of the macabre by having a pair of coffins discovered under the turf of the arena. When these were opened, out sprang two miraculously revived shin kickers from a bygone age – actually, a pair of Campden's younger latter-day citizens dressed up – who proceeded to give an impressive but not too painful demonstration of their barbarous pastime. Other sports included boxing, a marathon and a tug-of-war, followed by a bonfire and fireworks, but what made the night so memorable was a final torchlight procession into Campden, over a mile away, with the marchers headed by a pipe band. As the multitude of hand-held torches emptied into the streets of the old town, like a lava flow, turning the facades of houses into sheets of gold, children were lifted out of bed to see the wonder of it all and people with tears in their eyes said they had never seen anything to compare with it before.

The bonfire and torchlight procession were repeated on Coronation Day and the feeling grew in the town that there ought to be some annual observance on the hill. The National Trust, which owned the property, did not object, provided no mess were left behind, and after an interval of several years the games were revived permanently by a Robert Dover's Games Society and became one of my more spectacular annual assignments. Although the pattern rarely changed, I never got tired of attending the event, partly because Dover's Hill, itself, was such a joy to see: not so much a hill as a curving swathe of the Cotswold escarpment, where the land falls steeply to the Vale of Evesham, with views over Bredon and the Malverns to the darkling Welsh Mountains far beyond. Nature had here provided an effective amphitheatre with a level area, where the sports took place, overlooked by a semi-circular grandstand of moist turf, where hundreds of spectators could be accommodated. The sportsmen competed against a backcloth of the orchards and cultivations of the vale while overhead the sun would slowly sink into

Heigh For Cotswold!

a smoky twilight of evening: somehow the organisers never managed to get finished before dark! There was no more shin-kicking, though demonstrations were given of backswords, an equally obnoxious old sport in which contestants had to draw first blood by cracking open their opponent's heads with a wooden cudgel.

The approach to the hill was through fields of green corn, which seemed to sway to the music of the unseen pipers, playing over the hedgerow, where the hawthorn, now in full bloom, breathed a syrupy perfume. It paid to come well wrapped up because the wind grew colder as the light faded and the red and blue sweaters and anoraks of the myriad spectators glowed against the vivid green of the banks of the amphitheatre. The only warm people at the end of the evening were the competitors, whose arms and foreheads shone with perspiration. After the games, I could never tear myself away until I had seen the pipes and the endless, bobbing torchlight procession enter the town, which could be as late as eleven o'clock. The sight gave me the same thrill after thirty years as it had done when I first saw it in Festival of Britain year.

On the four hundredth anniversary of his birth, a wreath was laid on Robert Dover's grave at Barton-on-the-Heath, another place with a Shakespeare link. "Am not I Christopher Sly, old Sly's son of Burton Heath?" cries the tinker in "The Taming Of The Shrew". It was probably the first time Dover had been honoured on any anniversary of his birth or death, the wreath-laying and the memorial service preceding it, having been arranged by the Dover's Games Society.

The ubiquitous Seamus Stewart told the congregation that after Dover's death his games continued for two hundred years. The names of the people, who kept them going, had been lost in time but Dover's name survived and so had his joyful spirit, and it was this that had brought about a rebirth of the games in modern times.

Francis Burns, the society's secretary, said that Dover had been buried, aged seventy, in Barton churchyard 330 years before. "Who would have thought that all these years later, we should gather here to honour him or that the Olympic Movement of Great Britain would be so very interested in his games for what they represent?" he said. (Of recent years, representatives of the British Olympic Association had been in the habit of attending the Cotswold Games.) The wreath, consisting of a victor's laurel, decked with red carnations, was laid on Dover's grave with a card from the Dover's Games Society, saying,

"We will try to preserve the spirit of the Games", and I have no doubt they will for as long as the hill stands.

I did not get up early to go to work each day. There was no point. The majority of people I wanted to contact did not get to their offices till nine and wanted a chance to sort through their mail before being pestered by a reporter. Also, I had to work most evenings and felt entitled not to get up till eight when Mrs. Harvey called me. After listening during breakfast to what news she had heard from the neighbours or the milkman, I left for the office where my daily telephone calls to the police, fire brigade, etc, would be made. We had to keep a carbon copy, known as a "black", of all that we typed, so that we had something to refer to should a news envelope go astray on the train or copy be lost in the printing works. There was another, more personal advantage to this, too. If you picked up the paper on a Friday and saw a howler staring at you from one of your reports, it could be a relief to check the "black" and find that the error was not yours but the printers'. If, unhappily, it was yours, at least it gave you time to think up a plausible explanation before the editorial storm broke over your head!

I avoided drinking in the middle of the day if I could because unlike more hardened newspapermen I would become drowsy in the afternoon in consequence and unable to work properly. It was different after evening meetings though pub gossip was nowhere near as fruitful as that purveyed by the ladies, who were never wrong. In a small town or village they are all intuitive detectives. I would take a house-for-sale advertisement, published under a box number, and before you could bat an eyelid, the dames would have worked out which property it was and who was selling it and say to the "anonymous" vendor, "Oh, I see you're selling your house, then!" as a result of which he would descend on me, the only person apart from himself who was supposed to know, and accuse me of a gross breach of confidentiality.

Every district reporter, working on his own, needs an all-weather stand-by to fall back on when news dries up and mine was Moreton-in-Marsh duck pond, which safely saw me through many a silly season. "I see you've sent through another duck pond story," the Editor would say. "Short of news, are we?" But he always used it.

Once a person becomes a celebrity, anything he does is newsworthy be it never so trivial. The fact that he, whom everyone knows, has done it validates the story and all the journalistic embroidery that may go with it, and this was how it was with Moreton duck pond. Anything I wrote about it was news and found an audience among Journal readers because they all knew about the pond, which became a national cause célèbre during the mid-1950s, and though the world outside may soon have forgotten it, the local population had not. The peculiarity of the pond, which lay at the southern end of High Street and was completely devoid of ducks, was that it had two owners, one half belonging to Moreton Parish Council and the other half, to a private person. When the latter offered to buy the council's half in order to fill in the pond and build garages there, the council thought they would be getting rid of a liability and agreed to sell, but before doing so were obliged by law to call a public meeting to obtain approval for the sale of parish property, and this was where they came unstuck.

For the citizens of Moreton suddenly discovered an unsuspected affection for their muddy old pond and refused to part with their half of it. When the meeting was held in the town hall, the walls bulged with protesters and when the council tried to defend their action, several live ducks were let loose to flap overhead and quack their protest, too. A touch of xenophobia, rare for Moreton, occurred when a new resident, trying to put in a good word for the council, was tartly told by another speaker, "What do you know about it, gaffer? You ain't been in the place five minutes!" The outcome of the meeting was a near unanimous rejection of the proposed sale of half of the pond and a call for the council to resign, something that they not unexpectedly declined to do.

The duck pond affair was now taken up by Fleet Street, which saw it as a commendable example of the Britisher's determination to stand up for his rights. "The Times" published a donnish leading article about it and "Cassandra", of the "Daily Mirror", Britains best known columnist of the time, wrote wittily on the subject. Events had proved that while a government could dispose of an empire, a parish council, being closer to the people, could not part with half a duck pond so easily. The controversy ended when the private owner donated his half to the town, making the parish council the unhappy and reluctant owners of the entire pond. Their reaction was to tell the town, "All right! You wanted it and so you can do something about it because we won't!" and a duck pond committee was formed of which

All Over the Wold

I was founder member, but all our efforts to beautify the pond came to nothing. We dredged the mud but it silted up again. We removed dead branches but others fell in. We planted trees around it but they died. We introduced ducks to keep down the weeds but the birds had a habit of disappearing just before Christmas to end up in someone's pot. The pond refused to be anything but its perennially shabby self and the parish council had every justification for thinking, if not actually saying, "We told you so!"

Yet the duck pond, having achieved fame, became a true friend to me as a source of copy for all seasons. It flooded, it dried up, it froze and people skated on it, boys fell in it, ducks were put on it, ducks vanished from it, ducks died crossing the road from it, the R.S.P.C.A. investigated it, a Warwickshire man said something strange lay under it, swans settled on it, swans fought on it, including a brutal male which drove its adversary under the wheels of a passing car, moorhens bred on it, children fed the ducks on it, vandals tossed kerbing stones in it, citizens chafed at the sheer unsightliness of it, rates were spent on improving it, ratepayers raged at the cost of it... There was no end to the stories the pond provided! If news were short I always had the good old ugly duck pond to turn to for inspiration.

The months, the years, passed pleasantly by, annual assignments returning like old friends, and the more familiar they became, the easier they were to report. My life was like a calendar of events, beginning with annual general meetings, dinners and amateur plays in the winter; maypole dancing, bulb shows and gymkhanas in the spring; fêtes, flower festivals and barbecues in the summer, and horticultural and horse shows and harvest festivals in the autumn. Not everything was predictable, of course. Magistrates' courts and council meetings might take place at the same time and place, weekly or monthly, but what people did and said at them was never the same, and there were fires, crimes and accidents that no-one could foresee. Sometimes the truly extraordinary would happen, such as the Cotswolds' first visitation from Outer Space or so it seemed, even to a sceptic like myself.

I was working in the office when someone called to say that strange circles had appeared in a field belonging to Bill Edwards, who farmed at Evenlode, a village three miles away. I went over there and found what appeared to be half the population of the district heading in the direction of the field, which was in an isolated spot, well away from the road or any footpath or house. I joined the rest on foot and we made our way to the field, where we saw two circles imprinted on the grass, one inside the other. The outer circle was 23 feet across and the inner, 16 feet, and they were as accurate as if they had been drawn by a pair of giant compasses. The turf where they lay was indented and slightly discoloured, like the yellow left when objects are removed from grass on which they have stood a long time, and the inner circle was the more indented of the two. Neither Mr. Edwards nor any of his farming friends could account for the circles or recall having seen anything like them before, and on examining the ground, you were forced to the conclusion that they could only have been made by some large round object pressing extremely hard against the surface of the grass. In fact, if there were such a thing as a flying saucer, this was exactly the kind of impression you would expect it to make on landing. A U.F.O. expert arrived on the scene a day or two later but by then the lines had become too faint to be studied seriously and we were left with a riddle that no-one was able to solve either then or subsequently.

With mysterious objects allegedly flying the heavens, science fiction was all the rage and the subject of many books, films and television programmes. The B.B.C.'s "Quartermass" serials in which people turned into vegetables as beings from another world invaded the planet, had audiences glued to their television sets each week and accelerated the conduct of Cotswold meetings to a remarkable degree. On nights when an episode was to be screened, the proceedings would miraculously begin on time, the minutes of the previous meeting would be taken as read and the chairman would gallop through the rest of the agenda and barely pause at the end to allow "Any Other Business" before declaring the meeting closed, whereupon everyone would go haring home to his or her TV set instead of, as usual, in the direction of the bar. Only televised boxing or international football matches achieved a similar galvanising effect and not to be aware of what had happened on the box the night before was to disqualify you from conversation with your neighbours the following morning. The television age had well and truly arrived!

Despite this the Playhouse at Moreton-in-Marsh, the only cinema in the North Cotswolds, continued to thrive as it had done since its opening in the 1920s by George Thomas, a local man with a show business background. It was specially popular with Servicemen and women during the war and with their erstwhile enemies, the German and Italian prisoners, who were allowed greater freedom of movement after peace had been declared, including going to the pictures on their own.

An odd ritual used to occur each Easter when the manager had to apply to the Magistrates for permission to open on Good Friday, and not only that: she also had to give details of the film to be shown, a risible exercise because the beaks in those days knew nothing about what went on at the pictures. As long as it had a U for "Universal" certificate, which meant that it had been approved for all ages, they felt reasonably safe in letting it through.

The Playhouse did well because the local bus companies timed their services to coincide with its performances: moreover, passengers could buy their bus and cinema ticket combined and enjoy a ride, two hours at the pictures and the use of the cinema's comfortable foyer and snack bar, all for a modest sum, and they used to pour in nightly from all over the district, especially the young people. I used to say the cinema did more good in keeping kids off the streets than all the youth clubs in the area put together, and I am sure it would be operating still but for one thing: it suffered from the curse of Moreton-in-Marsh! Like the duck pond, it was split in two. One half belonged to one owner, the other half to another.

The late Mr. Thomas's family owned the original auditorium and rented it to a non-local firm, which had added the box office, lavatories, snack bar and foyer, and it was as a result of a disagreement over rent that the two parties fell out and the cinema closed. The family probably thought the firm was bluffing when it said it would prefer to move out rather than pay the rent required, and they also had a bit of a hankering to revive their show business past and run the cinema themselves, which was impossible, of course. The firm had installed a new wide screen and the latest projection equipment, which thus belonged to them and which they were perfectly entitled to remove on leaving, which they did. When the family moved in all they had got was a 1920s auditorium with screening equipment to match and there was no question of their being able to continue where the firm left off. The last film to be shown, was "The Spanish Main" remembered today, if at all, for its final shot of the lovers in the foreground and beyond them the sun rising boldly and improbably in the West!

CHAPTER FIVE

Royal Visits

ROYAL VISITS SOUND as though they ought to be difficult to cover but they were one of the easier assignments except, of course, for the photographers, who had only one chance to get the pictures they wanted. There was no opportunity for staging a photographic replay as sometimes happened when lesser mortals were involved. The reason was that what you could and could not do was clearly stated from the outset; you operated within well-defined but fairly generous limits, and there was usually no end of bumf issued to you about what the royal visitors would see and whom they would meet. You had almost enough information to be able to write your report beforehand. All that was left to be done was to watch out for the unexpected, which was unlikely to happen on such carefully rehearsed occasions, and, if the visitor was female, to say what she wore, something that put male reporters at a disadvantage, and the nearest available member of the opposite sex had to consulted.

Newspapers either got wind of imminent royal visits through local gossip or were officially informed by the Central Office of Information, and the Editor then hastily applied to the Newspaper Society in London for the carefully rationed royal rota passes, one pass for a reporter and another for a photographer. These passes, which allowed Pressmen to accompany the royal party, are issued by Buckingham Palace but allocated by the society, which weighs up the merits of the various applicants, then makes its choice, sometimes keeping editors in the dark till almost the last minute. A week before the visit no passes would have arrived, panic would set in, the Editor would telephone the Newspaper Society, then sigh with relief when the good lady responsible for sending the passes would say, "Don't worry, dear! Your passes will be put in the post tomorrow." Even so, the morning's mail continued to be ransacked until the coveted envelope, embossed with "The Newspaper Society", was delivered.

The North Cotswolds were rich in royal visits. Indeed, Moreton must have had more of them than any other town of its size in the kingdom. Edward VII stayed at Batsford House, as the guest of his friend Lord Redesdale, in 1905, and when out on a Sunday carriage ride, stopped and bought the "News Of The World" from an itinerant Campden newsvendor, Bob Dickenson, who thereafter bore the royal coat-of-arms on his satchel. Queen Mary, wife of George V, visited the Dugdale family at Sezincote House, near Moreton, and George VI inspected his troops assembled in the High Street in 1940, the bleak war-time atmosphere contrasting with the horse-drawn elegance of his grandfather's visit thirty-five years before. In 1974, Queen Elizabeth II opened the Fire Service Training College, the first institution of its kind in the world, created out of the former Moreton R.A.F. Station, and the Prince of Wales went there ten years' later as did his sister, Princess Anne, when she attended a charity ball in the officers' mess.

The magnet for the Royal Family, though, was the Central Flying School at Little Rissington R.A.F. Station, high on a hill above Bourton-on-the-Water, with sweeping views over Gloucestershire and Oxfordshire. The Queen Mother was the school's Commandant and her frequent visits were much looked forward to by the local Press, not only because of the pleasure of seeing her but because it meant two bouts of free hospitality in the officer's mess, where they were generous to a fault: the first, in advance of the visit to brief us about what would be happening, and the second, on the day itself. The C.F.S.'s famous aerobatic team, the Red Arrows, were based at Little Rissington and apart from being liberally wined and dined, we were also privileged to meet them and see both their dress rehearsal and their actual performance from a vantage point almost as favourable as that given to the royal visitor. In 1969, the Queen, herself, came to Little Rissington to present the Queen's Colour to the C.F.S., accompanied by the Queen Mother, the Duke of Edinburgh and Prince Charles, the biggest clutch of royalty ever to descend on the district.

A feature of these royal visits was the atmosphere of tension, firmly controlled but none the less there, that lasted till the royal visitors had gone, whereupon a gala-like informality would set in with smiles of relief all round and everyone letting his hair down. It was the nicest part of the day and you wished the royals could have shared it.

There was something very satisfying about having one of those rota passes hanging from your jacket lapel. Local bigwigs, who could sometimes look down their noses at the Press, were eager to be invited to royal functions and regarded themselves as fortunate even to get a seat in the back row. We disreputable reporters, on the other hand, were given choice positions from which to observe and record the proceedings, and if the royal visitors went on a tour of inspection, as they left through one door, we would be whisked off through another to watch from the next vantage point. The fact that faces which had just been left behind in one place, suddenly bobbed up again in another, did not seem to concern the visitors, who had no doubt cultivated the habit of not noticing this sort of anomaly. Sometimes the facilities were generous indeed. When the Prince of Wales came to Stow to open an old people's home and went on a walk-about in The Square, I was able to walk behind him, near enough to be able to hear what he said to individuals in the crowd, and when he moved off, I would grab their names before racing on to eavesdrop on the next conversation. Both he and his sister had homes in the Cotswolds by now and were looked upon not just as royal persons but as neighbours and friends. Princess Anne, the longer established in the area of the two, often took part in local equestrian events, displaying an informality rare, if not unique, in royal princesses. She would arrive driving her own horse box and if you stood in a queue at a hot dog stand, during a break between events, you might well find her queueing there too!

Of course, the worst could sometimes happen and we would not be given a rota pass. The understanding then was that any paper refused a pass had the right to call on one of its luckier rivals to supply as full a report as it published itself, together with a set of pictures, but this was a poor substitute for actually being there, especially if the other paper came out before you did, in which case all you had was material that had already appeared elsewhere. A galling aspect of some royal visits was that Fleet Street papers, who had bigger clout, would apply for and be granted passes, diminishing the chances of local papers, yet not bother to publish either a report or a picture if it did not happen to suit them. The worst humiliation of this kind occured when the Prince of Wales opened the Cotswold District Council's new headquarters at Cirencester in 1981, the council having been formed eight years earlier from an amalgamation of five smaller councils, including the North Cotswold Council. When the Prince arrived, Martin Vincent, of the Swindon Evening Advertiser, Gerry Stribbling, of the Gloucestershire Echo, and myself, the three who had reported the meetings of the new council since it started, had to stand outside in the road, along with housewives and flag-waving children, our respective newspapers having failed to secure passes for us, while strangers who had never set foot in the council chamber before, filled their notebooks and flashed their light bulbs to their heart's content because they boasted the coveted passes.

My most memorable royal visit was my first, which happened during the war, soon after I joined the Journal. At very short notice – it usually was in those days – we were notified that Queen Mary was to visit a Women's Land Army hostel at Medford House, a lovely eighteen-century mansion at Mickleton, which had been taken over since the war. We were invited to send a representative provided this report did not mention where the visit was, when it was or what the weather was like at the time, such being the security precautions in those days, and I was chosen for the simple reason that there was no-one else available.

When I set off from Evesham on my bicycle for the nine-mile ride to Mickleton the weather was excellent, as it had been all morning, and I did not bother to take a raincoat with me. By the time I had reached Bretforton, the sky had gone black and when I was halfway between there and Honeybourne, the rain started to pelt down. Faced with the choice of carrying on and getting soaked or sheltering and making myself late, I decided to shelter and thus got the worst of both worlds. After twenty minutes, I was late, the weather was no better and I had to carry on and get soaked anyway.

When I arrived at Medford House, I doubt whether I had ever looked such a mess. My grey flannel trousers were black from rain, my hair was plastered flat and droplets ran down my face and neck, soaking into my shirt and jacket. I don't think the policeman on duty outside the house would have let me in had I not had the official letter in my pocket and had he not seen me at Campden Magistrates' Court, which I was then beginning to cover regularly. The large vestibule was dark and empty and there was not a sound to be heard. My objective was to find somewhere as quickly as possible where I could attempt the nigh on hopeless task of tidying up my appearance. At the end of the hall, I had the choice of taking a passage either to the left or to the right. Alas! I chose the one on the right, and as I turned into it, I almost, but not quite, collided head-on with Her Majesty, who was just coming out.

I was suddenly aware of this familiar picture come to life: a silvery-grey presence standing before me with a distinguished looking man at her side and beyond, a mass of faces, the inmates of the hostel. It was the first time I had ever encountered anyone famous in my life! Queen Mary, wearing the inevitable tocque and ankle-length dress, was unperturbed, smiled at me and said, "Good afternoon, young man!" I have since thought of a dozen apt and courteous things I might have said in reply but the truth is I said nothing: I just gaped, ashamed of my dripping appearance and backed as hastily as I could into the hall from which I had just come.

There, I grabbed the first door handle I could find and shut myself in, my mind in a whirl at the thought of whom I had seen and that she had actually spoken to me. I stayed in the room for ages, not daring to come out till I felt certain the Queen had gone and that the coast was clear. It was not until then that I realised where I was. I had shut myself in the women's lavatory!

CHAPTER SIX

Centenarians, Etc.

WHEN I FIRST became a reporter, as a teenager, interviewing centenarians used to fill me with awe, not just because of the enormous difference in our ages but because I could not help thinking of all the famous people they could have known, like the Duke of Wellington or the Brontës, who seemed to belong not only to another age but almost to another world. As I grew older, the gap between their memories and mine narrowed and this sense of wonder faded but there still remained the fascination of meeting someone who had lived to a great age and pondering why they should have been chosen for longevity from so many. Although women are said to live longer than men, the twenty or so centenarians I interviewed over the years were equally divided between the sexes and came from no particular background. At least two were very rich while others were certainly very poor. If they had anything in common it was usually that they had a younger person to look after them and the companions often looked considerably older for their years than did the centenarians. Looking after the elderly is no sinecure. Much of their strength is drawn from those about them.

The first centenarian I interviewed in the Cotswolds was Mrs. Ann Udale, who celebrated her 103rd birthday in a primitive cottage in the village of Guiting Power, where she lived with a younger female cousin. She was sitting in a chair with her back to the window when I walked in, her silver hair very thin and her eyes, an astonishingly pale colour. After being interviewed on her 100th, 101st and 102nd birthdays, she knew exactly how to handle reporters and I soon began to wonder just who was supposed to be interviewing whom! She made up her mind that she was not going to talk about herself, the only subject I was interested in, and that she intended to dwell at length on her husband, a horticulturist, who had died many years ago and whom I was not interested in at all. I managed to extract from her the information that her health was good and that her only complaint was about getting up and down the stairs every day though I had to press her hard for answers to my questions. When I had finished, I rose and took leave of her, saying that I hoped I would see her again on her 104th birthday the following year or words to this effect. As I stood in the doorway, saying goodbye to her cousin, who was seeing me out, Mrs. Udale, not seeing very well, thought I had already gone and snapped, "These reporters! Always asking questions! Always poking their noses into other people's business! What a lot of Nosey Parkers they are!" and I motor-cycled home, feeling properly put in my place!

William Capers also lived to be 103. He, too, inhabited a primitive cottage, strangely known as Little London, in the village of Aston Subedge, which shelters under the slope of the Cotswold escarpment, near Campden. To reach his home you had to walk across a field from which could be seen an old orchard or two, with thicker woodland climbing up the hillside beyond. It was a lonely yet pleasant place, far removed from the hubbub of life. I first visited him on his 100th birthday and after making myself known to his wife, who must have been a good twenty years younger than he was, I was taken upstairs to find him in bed propped up against several clean white pillows. I gathered that he spent most of his time upstairs now and Mrs. Capers left me alone with him while she went on with her housework downstairs. I tried to conduct a conversation with him and he with me but neither of us succeeded in understanding the other, though I got the impression that he was trying to tell me about a ribald escapade of his youth when he had climbed up a ladder to a girls' dormitory. What was more disconcerting was that despite his age, he remained a well-made, heavy man and every so often he would start sliding towards me, gathering momentum as he went along, until I had to grab him at the last minute to prevent him from falling out of bed. Eventually we said nothing but sat in companionable silence with me grabbing him each time he started to slide and pushing him back on the pillows again.

We followed roughly the same procedure during the next three Decembers when I visited him on his 101st, 102nd and 103rd birthdays. He never went out of his room and as I was doing a good deal of youth hostelling in those days, getting to know the country, I thought how lucky I was to have seen so many places since we last met, while all he had to look at was the ceiling and walls of his bedroom. Only on one occasion did we briefly get through to each other. A little bird hopped on to the window sill and he pointed and said, "Robin!" and I replied, "I like robins. They come to cheer us up in the winter," and he smiled and nodded. Mrs. Capers, who, I had learnt, was his second wife, told me the old man loved having visitors but rarely saw anyone because the cottage was so cut off, and I mentioned this in my report, hoping that, perhaps, more of the villagers would take the trouble to call.

Soon after my report appeared, I got a telephone call from the Editor to say that another William Capers, aged 76, who lived in an old people's home at Stratford, had appeared on the scene. After seeing my report, he claimed that the older William was his long-lost father, whom he had not seen since emigrating to Australia at the age of seventeen. A meeting was to be arranged between the two Williams at Little London Cottage and I was instructed to be there to report what transpired. Mrs. Capers was nonplussed and sceptical, saying that her husband had never said anything to her about having a son by his previous marriage. The old man himself was too incoherent to confirm or deny the claim.

On the Saturday when the reunion took place, a cluster of reporters, including a B.B.C. representative with a microphone, descended on the cottage, which had not been so crowded in years. The younger William arrived in a taxi, hired by well-wishers, and was nothing like the older William in appearance. He was tall, stooped and thin with a sharp nose and droopy white moustache, whereas his alleged father was round-faced, an aged and somewhat shrunken John Bull. The two men were introduced upstairs with us reporters looking on, and old William, still propped up in bed, shook hands with his visitor for the benefit of the photographer. If the old man had lacked company before, he certainly did not do so that afternoon with a full bedroom and other people downstairs, waiting their turn to come up.

After the two men had sat together for a while and done their best to communicate, the younger William conceded that he must have been mistaken and this was not his father after all. "But I'm sure there must be something between us because we get on so well," he said. He had been given a pair of slippers to present to the old man, not the most appropriate gift for someone who was bedridden, nevertheless the thought was there, and after handing them over, he went downstairs to return to the taxi. As he was walking across the field, I caught up with him, told him who I was and asked, "Are you sorry the old man was not your father, Mr. Capers?"

A mischievous look came into his eyes. "Sorry?" he said. "What is there to be sorry about? I've had a lovely day out. The old man has had more visitors than he's had for ages – and you said yourself he liked having visitors. And you and the other reporters have got a good story for your papers. What is there to be sorry about?" And he then gave me a blatant, unmistakeable wink, which as far as I was concerned meant only one thing. The old boy had fooled the lot of us and had known all along that old Mr. Capers was not his father. But he was right, of course! We were, indeed, all the better off for his visit!

Golden weddings were fairly uncommon in my younger days and I used to go to some pains to ask the couples to account for their long and happy married lives together, but as the years went by and the effects of the Welfare State were felt, with older people being better looked after and living longer, a golden wedding became almost a commonplace, deserving only peremptory coverage. In any case, it was never the report that interested the couples but having their photograph taken, and sometimes when they discovered that I was only the reporter, they would get quite nasty about it and hardly spare me the time of day. They were mollified when I told them that I would be arranging for a photographer to call in due course but still felt peeved at having got all dressed up for an appointment with a mere reporter.

Diamond weddings, however, continued to be rare. To be married for sixty years meant the couples had to be eighty or more and there was less chance of both surviving to this age. Because I remained in the Cotswolds for so long, I occasionally had the experience of interviewing a couple on their diamond wedding day, ten years after I had been to see them on their golden wedding anniversary. One such pair was Sam Weaver and his wife, who lived at The Oaks, near Evenlode, and who aged not a whit, either of them, between the two anniversaries. Mr. Weaver, a lean and upright man with a rosy face and snowy hair, had been a farmer all his life; his wife, shorter and plumper, was a typical countrywoman, who doted on her husband and preferred to sit back and let him take the centre stage. Like most farmers, Mr.. Weaver was canny over money, kept a careful record of income and expenditure and would bring out bills he had hoarded for thirty or forty years to laugh at the way prices had changed since then.

When I called on the Weavers on their golden wedding day, I went to the back door having found that most people visiting farms proceed in this direction, and the couple asked me in and led me through the kitchen into the front parlour, where I was given a cup of tea. After I had finished interviewing them, I got up to leave, telling them not to bother to see me out: I could find my own way. I re-crossed the hall into the kitchen and had just reached the back door when Mr. and Mrs. Weaver, who had decided to follow me after all, entered the kitchen. Turning to wave goodbye, I simultaneously opened the door and stepped out, only to find myself disappearing down a flight of steps and landing on my bottom in the Weavers' pantry! I had chosen the wrong door! This was bad enough but I then had the humiliation of re-emerging into the kitchen in order to make my exit through the proper door. I had often heard the expression, "open-mouthed with astonishment" but had not actually observed this condition till I saw it written on the Weavers' faces as I came out of their pantry. The couple were flabbergasted! I apologised for my mistake, assured them that no damage had been done, either to their pantry or myself, and then got out by the right door as quickly as I could with scarcely a shred of dignity to wrap myself in. When I returned to see them ten years' later for their diamond wedding, they reminded me of the incident and we all had a good laugh about it.

Ernest Prew, a farm worker, and his wife, Priscilla, were married at Snowshill and went straight from the church to a cottage on the Springhill Estate that was to be their home for the next sixty years. A more isolated spot could hardly be imagined. They lived deep in the woods, over a mile from the nearest road, and when I went to see them for their golden wedding, the house had still not been connected to the electricity. When I returned after ten years for their diamond wedding, a supply had been laid on but Mrs. Prew's health had deteriorated in the meanwhile and she was less able to enjoy the electricity than she would have done at one time. As it happened, not only was she ill in bed but so was her husband, who was recovering from influenza, and this set me a problem because I had brought the Journal photographer with me and did not like to send him home empty-handed. It was a question of whether to waste the photographer and miss the chance of a picture or inconvenience the poor old Prews, and, shamefully, I opted for the latter alternative. While Mrs. Prew's daughter got her out of bed and sat her on a bedroom chair, I helped Mr. Prew put on his clothes over his pyjamas, so that he could sit beside his wife for a photograph, and with the two invalids propped together, doing their best to smile at the camera, the photographer took his picture, which turned out to be one of the happiest diamond wedding photos he had ever taken. No-one seeing it would have guessed that the radiant couple had just been lifted out of their sick beds and put back there immediately afterwards!

My experience with a third couple was less agreeable. On their golden wedding day I was particularly struck by the wife, who was a delightful little woman, sweet of face, neatly-dressed and graceful of manner. To be honest, I thought she was too good for her husband, who seemed a taciturn, ordinary sort of man to me. There was a bowl of roses in the centre of a large polished table and I remember thinking that the woman looked rather like a rose herself.

Therefore, when the couple reached their diamond wedding, I returned to the house looking forward to seeing her again, the first time for ten years. The husband, who answered the door, had not changed at all and led me into the sitting room, which was in use as a bedroom and no longer spick and span but decidedly untidy. On a rumpled bed in the corner lay a nightdressed figure whom he introduced as his wife, though I would never have recognised her. Her hair was dishevelled, her face bloated and her eyes dark and wild. Years of pain and illness had taken a terrible toll of her and she had the look of an angry, frustrated animal. I had stepped into the room smiling but her appearance came as such a shock that the smile vanished and I stared hard at her wondering whether it could really be the same person. I could have kicked myself afterwards for being so tactless because she spotted my reaction immediately. "Yes," she said bitterly. "I've changed, haven't I? Take a good look at me! This is what old age does to you! This is what getting old means!" Then, lifting herself up and glaring in my face, she hissed, with all the malice she could muster, "But don't feel sorry for me, young man! The same thing will happen to you one day!"

CHAPTER SEVEN

Shakespeare

I HAVE ALWAYS felt that the Royal Shakespeare Theatre belongs to me. The old theatre was burned down in the year I was born and thus the new theatre and I grew up together. It was there that I saw my first pantomime, first opera, first ballet and first Shakespeare play, a matinée performance of "Richard III" for which we queued, sitting on funny canvas-topped stools provided by the management. It was there that my form went prior to the School Certificate examinations, to see "The Merchant Of Venice", our set play for the English Literature course, and while boating on the river beforehand, I dropped my fountain pen overboard, an irreplaceable possession in those war-time days, and had to go through the exams with an ordinary pen dipped in ink. Full fathom five my fountain pen may not have lain but drowned in Avon it was, a platignum gleam wrapped in water weed on the river's bed. And it was to the theatre that I went as often as I could after moving to the Cotswolds, where the Royal Shakespeare Theatre is regarded not so much as a national institution but rather as the local rep. Likewise, the farmers of the Cotswolds and their families look upon Stratford not as the Birthplace but as a workaday country town, where they go to market and do their shopping every week. Shakespeare is merely a background figure to them.

But not, of course, to the multitude of foreign visitors who pour into the town each summer to visit the Birthplace and see the plays; and when a traveller has crossed half the globe, he wants to see a Stratford coinciding with the romantic picture of the place he has already formed in his mind's eye. To their credit, the Stratford tradespeople are determined to see that he gets it. Cafés are profusely half-timbered and Tudor named, curios cluster behind glass-bubbled shop windows and traditional flowers nod from window boxes. It is true that some of the display windows are filled with gimcrack souvenirs but they are no worse than those of any great tourist centre abroad and the sentimental value of these inexpensive bits of glass and plaster to a once-in-lifetime visitor should not be underestimated.

I still cherish a small mass-produced bust of Shakespeare given me on my first visit to Stratford.

The appeal that the Royal Shakespeare Theatre has for people from overseas was well-demonstrated by an encounter I had while attending an evening performance there, again of "The Merchant Of Venice". As my seat was in the middle of a row, I had to disturb a number of people to get to it and on reaching my place, found that I had, sitting on my left, an elderly, distinguished-looking woman and, on my right, a dark-complexioned young man, who obviously came from somewhere out East. He asked me awkwardly how much a programme cost and when I told him, he jumped up and made attempts to attract the attention of the usherette, but she was too busy showing latecomers to their seats. Nor, if she had seen him, could she have given him a programme because, as I have already said, we were in the middle of a row.

The young man was becoming so agitated that, in order to calm him down, I told him to give me the money and said I would fetch him a programme. He was clearly unaccustomed to going to the theatre and I think he appreciated my help. I rose to return back along the row, which I had just negotiated, but this was too much for the elderly woman on my left. "I simply can't keep getting up and down like this! Can't he borrow my programme?"

The young man excitedly replied, "No, I wish to take programme home as... as... souvenir!" and looked anxiously at me, whereupon I decided to press on regardless along the row.

"Really, this is most tiresome!" exclaimed the woman, struggling to her feet. "Some people have no consideration for others!" The rest of the people along the row also gave me disapproving looks as they made room for me to pass by.

After obtaining a programme, I hurried round the back of the stalls and approached my seat from the other end of the row, where I had fortunately not disturbed the people before. At last I reached my seat, sat down and handed over the programme to the young man, who thanked me very much.

The woman on my left now leaned towards me and said in a more conciliatory tone, "They ought to leave more room in theatres so that you can move along a row without disturbing other people." Since she was obviously trying to be pleasant, I agreed that it would be a good thing and then went on to ask the obvious question, "Is this your first

All Over the Wold

visit to the Royal Shakespeare Theatre?"

She said she had been coming to the theatre for thirty years. She visited Stratford each time she was on holiday in Britain, her home being in India.

"Do you think he comes from India?" she whispered, nodding in the direction of the man on my right.

"I'll ask him if you like," I said, feeling that I could be forgiven this liberty in view of the fact that I had fetched him a programme. "Do you come from India?" I said. "Yes," he replied.

Before I could get another word in, the woman leaned across in front of me. "How extraordinary!" she said. "So do I! Where do you come from? I have lived in several places. Do you know Poona, Delhi or Bangalore?"

With this last name she hit the nail well and truly on the head. The Indian's eyes lit up. "I live in Bangalore," he said. "Good Heavens!" replied the woman. "So do I!"

At this juncture the lights went down and the play began, but when the interval came, the two heads, one grey and the other dark, met above my lap as their owners engaged in animated conversation. She said she worked for an English mission in India; he said he was a teacher. They discussed mutual acquaintances and agreed to look each other up on their return. He was going back in two weeks' time. She was going back in January.

I could see I was de trop and asked to be excused. Outside in the foyer I recalled how on a previous visit to the theatre I had shared the same hand towel in the men's lavatory with the war hero, Field Marshal Bernard Montgomery, and been literally spat in the eye by the leading actor, Charles Laughton, declaiming on stage while I was sitting perilously close in the front row, and thought to myself that remarkable things could happen at the Royal Shakespeare Theatre!

When the quatercentenary of Shakespeare's birth took place in 1964, the Journal published a souvenir supplement to which I was invited or, more accurately, instructed, to contribute, the choice of topic being left to me. I remembered an old jingle, attributed to Shakespeare, which went:

"For I have drunk in
Piping Pebworth,
Dancing Marston,
Haunted Hillborough

> Hungry Grafton,
> Dodging Exhall,
> Papist Wixford,
> Beggarly Broom
> And Drunken Bidford"

and decided to go round the villages concerned to see whether they still lived up to their reputations today, and make this subject of my article.

My first call was at "Drunken" Bidford which clearly no longer deserved its tippling reputation. The police could not recall having a single case of drunkenness there, all the licensed houses being, to use the official phrase, "generally well-conducted", and the town appeared a model of sobriety. There used to be sixteen pubs in Bidford at one time but now there were only five, though the population was far larger than it had been. A resident told me she remembered no drunkenness since the war though one or two might occasionally get "market merry", as she put it.

At first Broom looked far from "Beggarly", being dominated by a thriving flour mill, and the postmistress told me she doubted whether there were any hard-up people in the village apart, perhaps, from an old-age pensioner or two. Nevertheless I found there to be a rather mean look about Broom, which did not strike me as being an attractive village. The hedges and verges were not as neat as they might have been and the church looked insignificant and untidy from the outside, though I must confess that when I reported all this in the paper, there was a very angry response from Broom, with dissenting letters pouring in for weeks, and I dared not set foot in the village again.

"Papist" Wixford might have got its name because it was owned by the recusant family of Throckmorton in Shakespeare's day. Another explanation could have been that as early as the tenth century, the village was given to the monks of Evesham Abbey by one of the Saxon Earls of Warwick. When I called, there was not a Roman Catholic living in the place. The inside of St. Milburga's church had a well-scrubbed Protestant look and there was no odour of incense, just the slightly musty smell you associate with remote old churches. A piscina and some fragments of old glass were reminders if its Papist past but otherwise church and village were indomitably C. of E.

Unlike Wixford, "Piping" Pebworth still had something to support its reputation. The village was said to have got its name because of its inhabitants' mastery of the pipe and tabor and there was a tradition that Shakespeare heard the village band play in the old Guildhall at Stratford. Pebworth still had its pipers but the oldest of them was only aged eleven! For the band consisted of the children of the village school, who were taught to play the recorder, presumably an acceptable substitute for the pipe, and regularly performed at school concerts, carol services and other occasions.

Alas! At the neighbouring village of "Dancing" Marston, the terpsichorean art had all but vanished. Occasional dances were held in the village hall for which a dual-purpose band would play "beat" music for the young and more sedate airs for the older dancers, but that was all. Gone were the days when the Marston Morris were renowned throughout Warwickshire for their prowess!

Another village no longer living up to its old reputation was "Hungry" Grafton, possibly so-called because of its stony, infertile ground though there is also a legend that Shakespeare was once refused a meal at the local inn. There was no need for either young or old to go hungry in Grafton when I called. School meals were provided for the children in the canteen of the village school and a "Meals on Wheels" for the elderly and housebound called twice a week.

There is no denying that "Haunted" Hillborough had a ghost. It once walked at Manor Farm where, so I was told, two farm hands were sitting in the kitchen late at night, one lambing time, when a female phantom appeared, scaring the life out of them. When one of the men ran upstairs to inform the master of the house, who was in bed, the latter impishly replied, "Why don't you send her up to me?" Cranhill Corner, near the hamlet, was believed to have been the site of a hangman's gibbet and at one time people would not go near it after dark. But Shakespeare might not have been thinking of ghosts and hangmen when he described Hillborough as haunted. Manor Farm was the home of Anne Whateley, the girl whom he is believed to have really loved and whom he was prevented from marrying by the untimely need to make an honest woman of the pregnant Anne Hathaway. Perhaps Shakespeare meant that for him Hillborough was haunted by memories of a lost love.

Finally, I came to "Dodging" Exhall, the village with the most difficult nickname to explain. Some said it was because Exhall was out of the way and difficult to find; others, that it was because of the long, winding village street, which "dodged" in and out. Whatever the explanation, the village successfully dodged the local bus service and there was no regular public transport to or from the village at all and I was glad to have my own car!

But was the author of the rhyme really describing Exhall as such? Perhaps he was referring not to the villages but to drinking cronies who came from them. Thus, "Dodging" Exhall might have been someone from the village, who dodged paying his round; "Beggarly" Broom, an inhabitant who always pleaded poverty, and so on. Whether or not Shakespeare invented the jingle, all the people I met knew immediately what the alleged characteristic of their village was without having to be reminded of it, and seemed quite proud of it, whether the description was flattering or not.

CHAPTER EIGHT

The Law

ONCE UPON A time, before the Wicked Fairy, Nationalisation, waved her wand, a small gas works stood at Stow-on-the-Wold, whose gasometer swelled with vapour and whose tall chimney uttered smoke. All the functions of this modest enterprise were performed by a single employee, who combined the roles of manager, office clerk, stoker, maintenance engineer and meter reader. His working hours were as comprehensive as his duties. When the town was running low on gas, he had to work late to boost the supply and when a housewife found her stove was not working, she immediately sent for him to put it right, no matter what the hour of day.

After nationalisation, the old works fell into disuse, the coal sheds were emptied of fuel and the reserve gasometer collapsed. All the gas came up from Cheltenham and there was no need for a supply to be manufactured in Stow any more. The old gas works were demolished but "Men are we and must grieve when even the shade of that which once was great has pass'd away." Several years before demolition, Stow gas works were involved in a case that made legal history, at least as far as the gas industry was concerned. At the beginning of January 1948, the siphon pipe of the gasometer failed, the holder had to be emptied and it was necessary to dig down eleven feet to get at what proved to be a break in the pipe. The result was that the town was without gas for a month.

In May of the same year, the private company owning the gas works, were summoned before the Stow Magistrates for "supplying in a main gas at a pressure which failed to balance a column of water not less than two inches in height." The prosecution contended that the company had broken the law by supplying gas deficient in pressure. James Hill, a local solicitor, who defended, submitted they could not have broken the law because they had supplied no gas at all. The Bench took the prosecution's view and imposed a fine but when the company appealed at the Quarter Sessions, Mr. Hill's submission was upheld and the appeal was allowed with costs. Thus, it was established that a gas company supplying no gas cannot be guilty of supplying gas deficient in pressure.

On this occasion the Stow Magistrates erred but this was the exception: they were far more likely to be right than wrong, and their disposition was to be too lenient rather than too severe. If they returned looking grim-faced and angry, after privately discussing what should be done with an accused, this was a good sign because it meant they were going to let him off with a good talking to. If they came in looking shifty and embarrassed, this was a bad sign because it meant they were going to send him down, something that as compassionate people they did not like having to do. They sat in a lofty, timber-vaulted courthouse built in the nineteenth century when Gothic architecture meant more than creature comfort and the place was a nightmare to heat. An antique, bulbous iron stove managed to grill all those within a yard of it but left everyone else frozen, and the modern convector heater chosen to replace it, certainly kept the place warmer but deafened everyone with its noise. With that church-like roof and large traceried windows at either end, the accoustics were atrocious, and when the wind was blowing hard, as it often did at Stow, pounding against the courtroom walls, accurate reporting of what was being said was difficult because it was so hard to hear.

Judge Alister Hamilton, who used to share the courthouse with the Magistrates for his quarterly County Courts, interrupted the proceedings on one such blustery morning by remarking, "The reporter obviously can't hear a word that's being said. He had better come up here and sit with me," which I duly did, savouring every moment of this unexpected elevation to his side. With the advocates face on, instead of speaking with their backs to me, as they had been, I was able to hear better than I had ever done in the court before. Though generally acerbic of manner, Judge Hamilton seemed to have a soft spot for the Press and was always good for a "quote", which he tended to aim straight in our direction. For example,

Judge (of an unemployed debtor): "What's the matter with him?"
Witness: "I believe there is some mental weakness."
Judge: "I've always understood a good day's work to be the best remedy for that condition. The medical term is 'occupational therapy', I believe."
Witness: "He also suffers from blood pressure."
Judge: "Indeed? Everyone's got that in one way or another."

There was nothing aloof about the Magistrates. They used to give me lifts to the court in their cars when my motor cycle was out of action, and when I finally bought a car, I would give them lifts in mine should the need arise. Inside the court, of course, things were different. Due deference had to be observed. We stood when they entered and sat when they sat and some of the more obsequious solicitors would bow to them deeply from the waist, but this did not mean that their word literally was law or that they were always unquestioningly obeyed. Take the case of Miss Emily Bough, aged 72, who appeared in court looking as though she had just stepped out of a Victorian picture album, a little white-haired lady dressed all in black. She was on remand from a previous court at which she had been found guilty of obtaining credit by fraud. It was stated that she kept getting accommodation at local hotels and boarding houses without having the money to pay. After discussing privately for over an hour what should be done with her, the Bench entered the court and the following dialogue took place.

The chairman, Lieutenant-colonel John Godman, to Miss Bough: "You have quite clearly been getting credit for accommodation when you had no reasonable hope of being able to pay for it."
Miss Bough: "I disagree. I had every hope of being able to pay."
The chairman: "Obtaining credit in this way is an offence for which you can be sent to prison."
Miss Bough: "I was not aware of that."
The chairman: " Please listen to me! You have the opportunity of going into an old people's home where you will be very well looked after. The only other alternative is to send you to prison because as far as we know you have no means of subsistence, except by getting credit for which you cannot pay. If you were to step out of this court at this moment, we don't know where you could go or how you could live except by obtaining credit. The court are prepared, if you will agree to it, to put you on probation on condition you agree to reside in an old people's home which we will find for you."
Miss Bough: "For how long?"
The chairman: "For a year, at any rate. If you don't agree to this, the court will have no choice except to send you to prison."
Miss Bough: "For how long?"
The chairman: "Probably for three months. We don't want to send a person of your age to prison. We would far rather overlook the offences you have committed and see that you are comfortably looked after in an old people's home. It is for you to say whether you will agree to be put on probation on condition you remain in the home."
Miss Bough: "Can you tell me whether it is lawful for a landlady to retain the

luggage of a person who has left without paying her bill?" (Miss Bough's luggage was at the Swan Hotel, Moreton, where she owed £10.)

The chairman: "As far as I know it is, but that has nothing to do with the case."

Miss Bough: "Of course it has! How long can she retain it?"

The chairman: "I should say until the bill has been paid, but that has nothing to do with it."

Miss Bough: "Very well, then. I shall go to prison for three months. I would rather do that than go into an old people's home. I know exactly what that would be like."

The chairman: "I don't think you do. They are very different now from what they were twenty years ago."

Miss Bough: "They may be, but I would be afraid that my present good health would be injured and that conditions would be absolutely intolerable. I have been inside an old people's home which is supposed to be one of the best in England, and so I know what it's like. I have several relations occupying roomy farmhouses with only three in the family. Can you not bring some pressure to bear on them to give me accommodation?"

The chairman: "No, we have no power to do that. Only very near relations can, in some cases, be compelled to take this action."

Miss Bough: "Very well, I will go to prison."

The chairman: "Are you quite sure?"

Miss Bough: "I certainly would not wish to be placed on probation in any case."

The chairman: "I think you are making a big mistake."

Miss Bough: "And I am sure I am not!"

The chairman: "Well, you give us no alternative. The sentence, then, is three months' imprisonment."

Miss Bough, who had no previous record, then left the court accompanied by two policewomen. I gather that she soon adapted the prison to her requirements and had the wardresses firmly under her thumb, and naturally, it had not escaped her notice that three months in prison was a great deal shorter than the twelve months or more on probation in an old people's home!

In 1961, a Cirencester solicitor, Peter Sanders, achieved the distinction of prosecuting and defending in the same case at Stow court: a case in which a bus driver was accused of driving his vehicle without due care and attention. For the prosecution, Mr. Sanders said the man drove his bus out of a side road into the path of a car on the main road, causing a collision. He had seen the car but thought he had time to get across in front of it.

After completing the case for the prosecution, Mr. Sanders went on to say that the bus driver's solicitor had been prevented from getting to the court, due to a last minute hitch, and had asked him to say a few words on behalf of the accused. Deftly switching from prosecution to defence, Mr. Sanders explained that if the brakes on the car had been more efficient, it would have been able to pull up in time to avoid the bus. The accused man had been driving twenty-five years and had no previous convictions, despite clocking up a heavy mileage each year. After such persuasive arguments, both for and against him, from Mr. Sanders, the bus driver, who had pleaded guilty, got off with a £15 fine.

An example of how the law must take its course, once put into motion, was provided by a case of theft at a small village near Stow. A woman noticed dirty footprints on her bedroom carpet, checked a cash box inside her dressing table, found £17 in notes to be missing and reported her loss to the police. While examining the woman's home, the police found a pair of muddy shoes which exactly fitted the footprints on the floor. The shoes belonged to her son, aged seventeen, who was questioned and admitted being the thief. He apologised to his mother and promised to pay the money back. The woman understandably wanted the case to be dropped but the law having being put in motion had to take its course, and the boy appeared in court, charged with stealing, and was put on probation for two years.

An embarrassing task for a reporter covering courts was having to reject the pleas of convicted people for their names to be kept out of the paper. I was told heartrending stories about the effect my reports would have on the health of sick relatives or the attitude of puritanical employers but I could not set myself up as some kind of umpire to decide who should suffer opprobrium and who not. Apart from the ethical side of it, I could also jeopardise my own future if I were found to have suppressed a report, and there was always a suspicion that the individual concerned, having achieved his object, would then go around bragging, as he most likely would, that he had "fixed" the Press to his advantage.

When supplicants became excitable or nasty I had to refer them to the Editor, knowing full well that they would get nowhere with him and would virtually be guaranteeing that a report appeared, all in the good name of integrity. My strongest card in the early days was explaining that the Journal reported all the court cases, which was a fact, and that we could not make exceptions, but as the years went by it became less and less true, mainly due to the big increase in motoring offences. Cases involving drivers from other parts of the country, whose only connection with the Cotswolds was that they had chosen to collide with each other there, obviously had little local news value, and crime was also on the increase with the court lists running into several pages. For space reasons alone we were obliged to be more selective and focus on those cases with a strong local connection. The odd thing was that as we became more selective and thus on less surer ground morally, the fewer requests we received for court reports to be suppressed, the result, no doubt, of the times having become more permissive and the community more tolerant of others' transgressions. Certainly, as far as some of the teenagers were concerned, appearing in court and having their names reported in the paper, seemed tantamount to earning their spurs.

The Cotswold Coroner also shared the courthouse with the Magistrates for his inquests, which were kept as low-key and unemotional as possible to spare the feelings of those relatives of the deceased who had to attend. Only at inquests with a jury did formality break through in the form of an archaic preamble that needed a master orator to do it justice. It went:

"Oyez! Oyez! Oyez! All manner of persons who have anything to do at this court before the Queen's Coroner for this county… draw near and give your attendance, and if anyone can give evidence on behalf of our Sovereign Lady the Queen… let him come forth and he shall be heard, and you good men of this county, summoned to appear here this day to inquire for our Sovereign… answer to your names as you shall be called, every man at the first call upon the pains and perils that shall fall thereon!"

I used to wonder exactly what those pains and perils were that would fall on a juryman if he failed to answer at the first call! The unfortunate policeman required to deliver this declaration in front of the assembly, had not been speech trained or groomed by the Royal Academy of Dramatic Art and the result was a delivery so ill in its emphases that you felt more embarrassed than awed and relieved for his sake when it was all over. It was certainly an occasion when a policeman's lot was far from a happy one! Inquests were the easiest of all assignments to write up because the evidence unfolded in sequence, like a story with the Coroner's verdict its denouement, though the details were too sad or even gruesome, to make the task an agreeable one. Sometimes if they were a juryman short they would rope me in to make up the number.

My relations with the executants of the law, the Gloucestershire Constabulary, were always very good, which was more than I could say about the police of some adjoining counties. The Editor, who was equally impressed with them, once wrote a leading article, in which he said that as the British police were the best in the world, then the Gloucestershire police, who were the best in Britain, must be the best of all police forces, and I saw no reason to disagree with this opinion. Instead of trying to fob off reporters, they seemed genuinely keen to help and invited the Press to County Police Headquarters regularly to hear complaints and discuss improving relations with us. As for the Cotswold-based police, they not only kept me well-informed but did me innumerable acts of kindness, such as bandaging my leg when I fell off my motor cycle and regularly giving me a push when I bought my first, very unreliable secondhand car. Some of the bicycling young constables, who had been in the Cotswolds when I started, later returned to the district as middle-aged superintendents or chief inspectors in charge of the area and their astonishment at finding me still there would give me a nasty twinge or two about whether I ought to have made more of my life than I had so far.

CHAPTER NINE

Estates

IT HAS BEEN said that there are more millionaires living within ten miles of Stow than anywhere else in Britain outside London. Whether this is true is debatable but the district is undoubtedly wealthy and this is reflected in the large number of fine estates located there. In my time, Harry Ferguson, the tractor magnate, lived at Abbotswood, with its famous gardens; Lord Rothermere, the newspaper owner, at Daylesford, Warren Hastings's home, which he lovingly and expensively restored after its damaging five-year occupation by the military during the war; Sir Cyril Kleinwort, the banker, at Sezincote, with its oriental domes and Kubla Khan pleasure grounds; Lord Dulverton, of the Wills tobacco family, at Batsford, with its arboretum, possibly the finest in the kingdom, and the Earl of Wemyss, represented by his mother, Lady Violet Benson, at Stanway, perhaps the loveliest estate of them all, and these were by no means all the prestigious landowners in the area. Sometimes a whole village would belong to an estate, which may seem feudal to the townsman but the system worked advantageously for all concerned in the country. Large tracts of unspoilt landscape had vigilant protectors; noble houses were inhabited and well cared for, and the farms on the estate were let to yeoman tenants who would not have stood a chance financially of owning a farm of their own. The landlord presided in his mansion, enclosed by its elegant private park, while the outer territory was the demesne of the farmers, whose only obligation was to make enough money from their land and stock to pay the rent when it fell due. In my experience, the relationship between landlord and tenant-farmer was cordial, even affectionate.

When Captain Edward George Spencer-Churchill, owner of the Northwick Park Estate, celebrated his eightieth birthday, his twenty-eight tenant farmers presented him with a silver salver, on which each of their signatures was inscribed, and spoke warmly in praise of him. As the local reporter, I was invited to the presentation, which took place at a dinner at Northwick Park mansion, an event that I took some satisfaction in attending because I had been born in a brick terraced house built on Northwick land at Evesham and never dreamt that one day I would sit at table in the sanctum sanctorum of the family's dining room.

It was a touching, autumnal occasion with some of the farmers not far off eighty themselves and Charlie Dee, of Park Farm, who made the presentation, was among the most senior of them. "The average Englishman does not wear his heart on his sleeve," he said, "but there comes a time when it is good for everyone to say a little of what he thinks and feels. Captain Spencer-Churchill is not only our landlord but he has been a good friend to all of us who have occupied farms on this estate. As one who has been in the same farm for over forty years, I feel I can speak with some authority when I say I have never known him lack consideration for others, especially during the recent difficult times which we have all been through together." (He meant, of course, the war).

Proposing a toast to Captain Spencer-Churchill, John Galt, of Dovedale Farm, said, "Here at Northwick we enjoy the best landlord in the world, a gallant English gentleman who has loyally served this green and pleasant land through more troublesome times than I hope we shall ever see again, and it is good to find the old landlord-tenant system running so smoothly in this new nuclear age."

Clasping the salver, Captain Spencer-Churchill, a tall, slender silver-haired bachelor cousin of Sir Winston, replied, "It will certainly be a treasured possession for the remainder of my sojourn on this planet and if, in many centuries' time, it is dug up by some enthusiastic archaeologist, I can well imagine some Socialist saying, "Well, it looks as if that reactionary tenant-landlord system did sometimes allow goodwill between the parties and was beneficial to both."

After Captain Spencer-Churchill's death in 1964, his famous art collection was dispersed, two paintings from it by Beccafumi being acquired by the National Gallery; the estate was divided and the mansion, after being used briefly as a rehabilitation centre for drug addicts, became empty. When Mr. Dee and Mr. Galt died, the tenancy of their farms passed to their sons, thus preserving the families' link with the Northwick Estate.

The beautiful Norton Estate, near Campden, belonged to the Earl of Harrowby, whose heir, Viscount Sandon, occupied the family seat on the estate, an eighteenth century brick building whose name, Burnt Norton, provided the title for one of T.S. Eliot's poems. I once asked Lord Sandon, later the 6th Earl of Harrowby, what he thought of the poem and he plainly did not like it and, what was more, was suspicious about how Eliot came to be on the premises in the first place. When I jocularly reported in the paper that the poem might be a unique example of a literary work resulting from an act of trespass, we received a letter from Major Escourt Cresswell, of Charingworth Manor, near Campden, exonerating the poet.

"My mother living at Ardeley House, Chipping Campden (now The King's Arms Hotel), kept five-year diaries. These, together with her private correspondence, have disappeared, with the exception of the locked diary for 1934-38.

"Under Saturday, July 28, 1934, there is the entry '...Had the Americans, Perkins (my note, Dr. and Mrs.), Miss Hail and a poet, Mr. Eliot, to tea... Further entries that summer mention "...dinner parties with the Americans..."

"At this time, my father was running the shoot at Burnt Norton and neighbouring farms on behalf of the North Cotswold Hunt. The previous tenants were Birmingham businessmen who had caused a lot of bad feeling.

"In pursuance of my current ambition to become a gamekeeper, I took every opportunity of pestering the long-suffering Head-keeper, George Fawcett, and the kindly Mrs. Fawcett. During the summer I used to accompany my father on his Saturday visits to pay Fawcett his wages and expenses, discuss the running of the shoot and inspect the rearing pens.

"I can remember both my father and mother mentioning Eliot visiting Burnt Norton when the poem was published but, if as seems likely, my father took Eliot over after tea on July 28 I would not have been present, as I did not come back from school until July 31.

"While my father was dealing with Fawcett it is quite possible that Eliot wandered over to Burnt Norton house and gardens. Although the house gave the appearance of being unoccupied, the Dowager Lady Lincolnshire was living in one wing, and the shoot always took particular trouble not to disturb her. The entry must have been by chance!"

Burnt Norton acquired its bizarre name from a spectacular fire in which the then owner incinerated the property and himself with it. Sir William Keyte, a Member of Parliament for Warwick, was a classic example of the eighteenth century gentleman rake. After living with his wife at Clopton, near Stratford, for several years, he took an innkeeper's daughter as his mistress and went to live at Norton, a fairly modest place on the escarpment between Campden and the Vale, and frittered away a fortune on building a splendid new house and gardens there. As his debts grew and one mistress succeeded another, Sir William began to drink to excess, mortgaging the property to the hilt. Left alone in his fine new house, a bankrupt and an alcoholic, he put an end to it all on the night of September 9, 1741, when he was 53 years-old, by setting fire to various rooms with lighted candles and literally going up in flames. Only the modest house that had been there beforehand survived the blaze, a calamity described by George Ballard, a Campden scholar, in a letter to his mother, dated September 11, 1741.

"I suppose you have heard of the dismal misfortune at Norton," he wrote, "and imagining you would like some account of it, you may please to understand, that on Wednesday night, exactly at eight o'clock, a servant of Sir William Keyte's came riding furiously through the town, crying out that Norton House was on fire. I immediately ran thither, accompanied with a very great number of people, and to my no small affliction, saw the greater part of that beautiful house in flames, which was the most terrible sight I ever beheld; for before I came within view of the house, it seemed to me to be like Mount Etna, the force of the fire throwing up incredible quantities of smoke and flame a most prodigious height into the air. That part of the house facing Aston was preserved (I believe, by a partition wall) some considerable time before it was burnt, but before twelve o'clock, every part of that delightful house that was combustible, was consumed and reduced to ashes. Sir William set it on fire himself, and voluntarily burnt himself in it, which was a dispatch too speedy for such a monster, who ought, like Lodowick Grevil, to have suffered death more leasurely."

On July 23, 1953, I spent a day at Burnt Norton covering the bicentenary celebrations of the acquisition of the estate by Sir Dudley Ryder, grandfather of the first Earl of Harrowby, since when it had remained continuously in the family. Dinner was provided for the tenant farmers and cottagers in a marquee lighted by lanterns, calling to mind the traditional farm suppers and rural feasts of long ago, and the speeches were as appreciative as those at Northwick had been. Proposing a toast to the estate, Bill Organ, of Manor Farm, said, "This estate is in one of the most beautiful parts of the country and I congratulate Lord Sandon on his ancestors who bought it and my parents who came to it, and I hope that one day my children will say I was right to have stayed here. It is a big satisfaction to us that Lord Sandon has sons and that his sons have sons, and we can go back home tonight with the hope that the estate will stay in the hands of the family for ever."

Seconding the toast, Bert Ladbrook said, "There have been

Ladbrooks on this estate for generations: my father lived here all his life and my grandfather was estate foreman. According to the records, ours is the oldest surviving name on the estate, and there were Ladbrooks here even before Lord Sandon's family bought the property. Both Lord and Lady Sandon have always been good people to their tenants. They have taken an interest in the village, especially our church, and we cottagers are thankful to them for the improvements they have done to our homes. We couldn't have better landlords than Lord and Lady Sandon."

A word of praise for the tenants came from Bill Haynes, of Kingcombe Farm, who farmed on the estate for fifty-six years. "When you gets to eighty-eight, like me," he said, "you begin to feel something is a-coming on, and there is one thing I would like to tell Lord Sandon. I've been in my bed from January 14th to this day and I have thought things up and I reckon Lord and Lady Sandon have got the best lot of chaps in the world on their estate. I've reckoned it up and there's ne'er a boozer among them. They are all good chaps and real workers. We all know what things are like nowadays, but if life's not all honey and sunshine we must put up with it. I think the agricultural life is the best in the world. You gets good health and you don't have to trouble too much about the Government not allowing you to do this and that – I daredn't tell you all I knows! I was always treated the best way a man could be treated during the time I was on the estate, and I might even say I wish I was young again so that I might have fifty-six years with them all over again!"

Lord Sandon, a tall, scholarly-looking man, who came to the supper dressed in eighteenth century costume, including a long wig, said "Lady Sandon and I have loved every sod of soil on this estate. I have links with it that go back to the earliest days of my recollection. You can understand why we want to cling to it. The whole country is trying to stop us but we are going to try and keep it, come what may! We pray for God's blessing on this estate and whatever the future may hold, we must surely look back on the last two hundred years of the estate as a testimony to goodness and wise planning."

Lord Sandon was not allowed to end his days at his beloved Burnt Norton. When he succeeded to the earldom in 1956, he and Lady Sandon were obliged for practical and financial reasons to move to Sandon Hall in Staffordshire, the traditional seat of the Earl of Harrowby; Burnt Norton briefly became a boys' school, then like Northwick, became unoccupied though the latter was eventually turned into flats.

CHAPTER 10

Play Acting

ALL REPORTERS ON a weekly newspaper are expected to have a second string to their bow, a subject, such as golf, gardening or motoring, on which they are expert or moderately so and on which they can expatiate knowledgably in addition to their normal duties when required to do so for articles or book reviews. Mine was the Drama, the joker in the pack, because unlike the others, it involved lots of night work, attending amateur plays in makeshift theatres in uncomfortable village halls. To be fair, I also got free tickets for professional shows at the Everyman Theatre, Cheltenham; the Swan Theatre, Worcester, and, when our Stratford man was not available, the Royal Shakespeare Theatre, but even this was not unalloyed pleasure. It meant turning out when your inclination after a hard day in court or at a council meeting, might be to stay at home by the fire, then driving a fair distance in bad weather, thespian activity being greater in the winter than at the better times of the year, and finally, after enjoying the play or otherwise, having to sit down and write it up, knowing full well that your review would be read by others more expert than yourself who might challenge your opinions.

To state the obvious, there was a lot more to reviewing plays than just having a night out, then describing what you thought of the performance. The two professional repertory companies whose work I regularly saw, were always walking a tightrope financially and too much disparagement from the Press could lose them the confidence of their sponsors and the support of their customers to the detriment of the box office. On the other hand, I could hardly say a play was good if I thought it was not: this would have been unfair to our readers who like me had to turn out of an evening and drive some distance but unlike me, paid for their ticket. So I was also walking a sort of tightrope, trying to please the theatre by being constructive and respecting the readers by being truthful, and it was still necessary to make a review sufficiently interesting to attract the general reader as well as the theatre enthusiast.

Play Acting

There were three reasons why I dropped into the Journal's drama slot. (I hated being called the paper's drama critic because it sounded too grand for someone who was merely doing his best in what time he had left over from the rest of his reporting work.) First, I was known to be a keen, though not fanatical, playgoer, and secondly, I had taken part in amateur plays at St. Edward's Hall, Stow, where a temporary stage was hammered up in a building crammed with delicate Civil War and Restoration portraits, including a full-length reclining nude of Nell Gwynn at which it was hard not to stare whether off stage or on. Indeed, I had the unique and clearly not to be encouraged experience of once reviewing a play in which I, myself, appeared, the Journal having failed to find anyone else to cover the event, and I must have got away with it because no-one wrote questioning our impartiality! And, thirdly, I had produced one-act plays for Moreton Young Farmers' Club for their annual county talent competition, held in various parts of Gloucestershire. Anyone taking on the job of transforming young farmers into actors needs his head examining, but it could be a fascinating experience, seeing talent emerge from unlikely sources and though they were noisy, boisterous, late for rehearsals and slow to learn their lines, I always ended up feeling proud of them on the night. The worst part was the competition, itself, invariably held in unsuitable premises and culminating in an arbitrary adjudication by some has-been actor, making the most of his captive audience. We carried off the trophy once with an off-beat nativity play in which real shepherds played the shepherds, though I did not hear the result declared, being outside, as usual, pacing up and down the road.

Amateur drama is not as awful as tradition would have you believe though some productions are a great deal better than others. In particular, school plays, which come round each autumn term, just before Christmas, were full of zest and invention and provided some of the best theatre-going experiences I have had. Curiously, I was never bored by an amateur play yet I have dozed off more than once during a professional show, and this used to puzzle me a good deal because the latter was obviously better done. Admittedly, a proper theatre was a good deal warmer than some of the chilly Cotswold halls I had to sit in and I also had to be attentive at an amateur play, knowing that afterwards I would have to write it up. But the real reason, I believe, was that there was always an element of the

Mr. Garne and his "Cotswolds"
(Ch Heigh for Cotswold!)

The Pasque Flower
(Ch Heigh for Cotswold!)

In Chipping Norton's fire-gutted town hall 1950

The old trout (Ch Places)

Queen leads royal party at Central Flying School (Ch Royal Visits)

Queen at Moreton-in-Marsh Fire College (Ch Royal Visits)

At opening of Cotswold Farm Park 1971

With motor-cycle
(Ch Moreton-in-Marsh)

Mr. Harvey, Nip and Spot
(Ch Heigh for Cotswold!)

Pasolini directs "The Canterbury Tales" (Ch Play-acting)

As pall bearer with bell (Ch Play-acting)

Tree planting at Stow (Ch Heigh for Cotswold!)

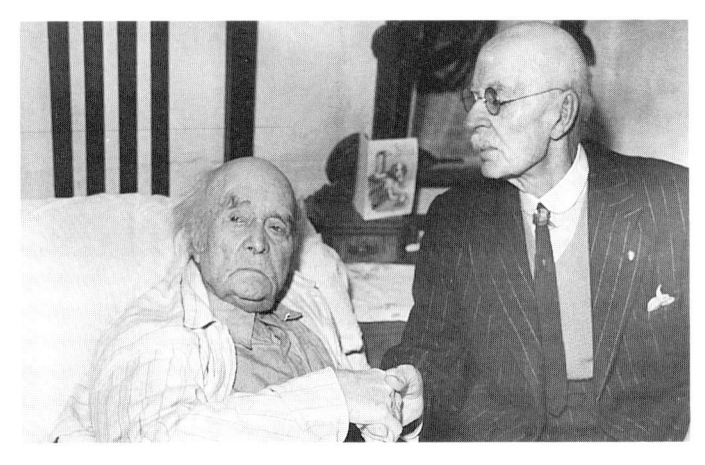

The two Mr. Capers (Ch Centenarians)

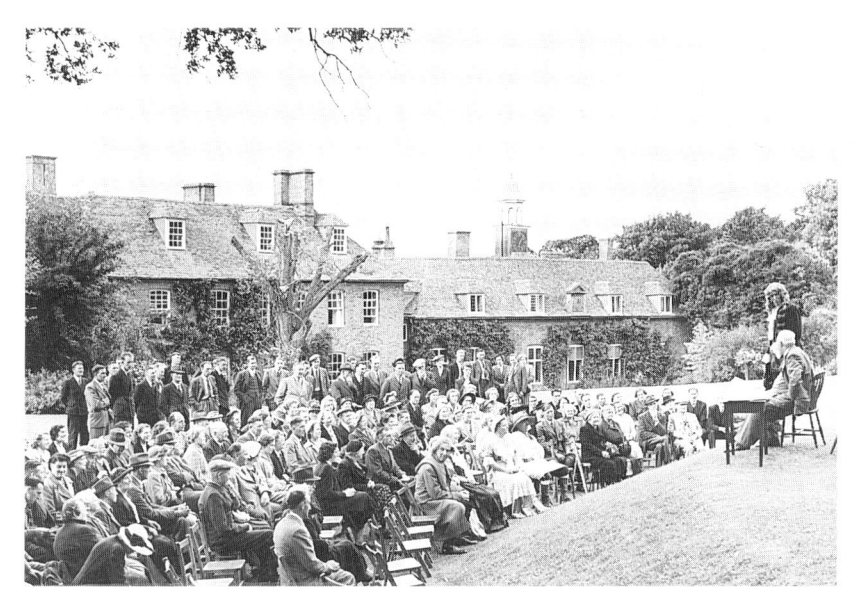

Burnt Norton Bicentenary (Ch Estates)

Capt Spencer-Churchill with his farm tenants (Ch Estates)

As Father Christmas (Ch Play-acting)

Young Farmers'
Prize-winning Play
(Ch Play-acting)

unpredictable about an amateur performance to keep you on the alert. When you went to see a professional performance you expected it to go smoothly and were surprised if it did not. With an amateur play, it was rather the reverse. You kept expecting things to go wrong and were pleasantly surprised when they did not, as no doubt the cast were, too.

For amateur players are very vulnerable to mishaps. We were always having trouble at Stow with the bellringers, who would insist on practising while we were giving a performance, drowning what was being said on the stage with their tintinnabulation, and it was not unheard of for the Fire Service to conduct a lightning raid on a hall during a performance to check that the safety regulations were being obeyed, including on the stage itself, where the cast had to carry on regardless, pretending the obtrusive fire officer was not there. I once fell victim to a stage mishap, myself, when someone in another part of the hall at Stow plugged a tea urn into an already overloaded electricity supply and fused the lights while I was alone on stage, doing a telephone conversation, which I then had to spin out in the dark till normality returned.

My worst theatrical experiences, however, were both off the stage. The women at Stow in charge of the make-up applied it far too liberally on we men, who could have got away with very little or none at all, and as the hall had no washing facilities, we had to go home in our greasepaint and get cleaned up there. While returning one night I had trouble with my motor cycle, a not unusual occurence, and was kneeling down beside the machine, trying to find what was wrong, when a car drew up and the driver got out, asking whether he could help. It turned out to be the local plain clothes policeman, the last person I wanted to see under the circumstances, and while he did his best to provide more light by turning his headlamps full on, I was desperately trying to keep my face averted to prevent his seeing my make-up, an adornment that I felt it beyond my capacity to explain.

J.P. Sartre's play, "In Camera", postulates the idea that Hell consists of being shut up for Eternity with other people. While reviewing a performance of the play at the Victoria Hall, Bourton-on-the-Water, I discovered a different but equally intolerable form of hell. Sitting in the back row, the hall being a very small one, I found myself behind a woman who kept fidgeting and talking to her next-door neighbour and decided to move to another empty seat but as I rose, a large trestle table, standing end-upwards behind my chair, lunged forward and landed across the back of my neck. It seemed that it was only my chair that had been holding it up. When I tried shoving it back with my head, it made a groan that caused several people in the audience to turn round. At a second, more determined attempt, it returned to its former position, then bounced back with an enormous whack against the back of my head, causing practically the entire audience to turn round to see what was going on. I realised that I had no alternative but to stay as I was until the interval, when I could free myself, and sat there rigidly, a prisoner of the table. When the interval seemed a long time in coming, I glanced with difficulty at my programme and saw with horror the footnote, "The play will be performed without an interval." So there I was, trapped for over two hours with a fidgeting woman in front of me and a heavy table top leaning on the back of my neck, unable to move a muscle without causing creaks and groans in an atmosphere in which you could have heard a pin drop, such was the power of the play! It was a long, long evening!

The closest I came to being involved in a professional production was on a magical autumn day in 1971, when the Italian director, Pier Paolo Pasolini, descended on Campden to shoot a sequence for his film of Chaucer's "The Canterbury Tales". In the space of a few hours on a Sunday morning, he and his team blotted out the present and gave the people of Campden a unique opportunity to see their town as it must once have looked, several centuries ago. The tarmac was buried under sand and straw, modern signs, shop fronts and other anachronisms were obliterated, the arches of the old market hall gleamed with jars, bottles, fruit and vegetables, and from as far as The Square, where a carthorse stood quietly beside a loaded farm wagon, to the Old Grammar School, where a wooden gibbet concealed a lamp-post, there was bustle and people, a medieval tapestry come to life. Children played, women went marketing, men carried firewood, sold bread and pushed barrows, nuns and friars walked, fires burned, geese waddled, sheep bleated and dogs barked, while helmeted soldiers vigilantly looked on. All the costumes were of quiet greys, blues and blacks, the colours of frugal, unassuming people.

I had heard that they were looking for extras and was signed on myself on the day prior to shooting, together with ninety-nine inhabitants of the town. (A week after the filming, a national newspaper reported that the actors' union, Equity, was angry because "locals" were hired instead of professional extras, and it was rumoured that Pasolini was dashing from one English location to another in order to keep one jump ahead of the union.) We were told to report to the Town Hall the next morning at six and when we did so, in the shimmering light of dawn, the women were taken upstairs to be fitted with their costumes while we men remained on the ground floor to be fitted with ours. A problem then and throughout the day was that none of the Italians spoke English properly and their instructions, when they came, were far from clear, prompting some ripe comments in reply from the Cotswoldians, who were not used to being jabbered at by a lot of dark-eyed, dapper foreigners.

I found myself being eyed up and down by one of Pasolini's henchmen, who pulled me to one side, together with another of the taller men, and indicated that we would be wanted to do something special. We were fitted out with heavy, deeply-hooded monks' robes and given perilously loose-fitting sandals to put on our bare feet, and I was also made the custodian of a large handbell. The two of us were then taken outside and made aware, more by gesture than anything else, that we would be required to walk the length of High Street carrying a "corpse" slung on a pole to be borne on our shoulders, I, as the first pall bearer, also having the task of simultaneously ringing the handbell. The "corpse" proved to be the actor, Robin Askwith, who was very friendly and bright despite being clad in only a thin pair of breeches with the remainder of his flesh covered in goose pimples because it was still quite cold. Nor did he seem daunted at having to be suspended head downwards from a pole and carried by a pair of funerary novices. The street was cleared and after a distant cry of "Action!" for we must have been a good two hundred yards away from the director and cameras, we began our plod down the street towards them, with me dolefully ringing the bell and doing my best not to trip over the sandals and the trailing hem of my robe or let go of Mr. Askwith. It was the first scene of the day to be filmed and there was an extraordinary stillness everywhere, except for the bell, and a thin mist momentarily came down to enhance the melancholy of the event depicted.

After repeating our journey for a second take, we rejoined the other extras to provide anonymous figures in the crowd for the big market sequence that occupied the rest of the day's shooting. By mid-morning, the sun had come out to provide impeccable autumn weather with the golden buildings glowing in the light. As the word

Play Acting

got round, crowds began pouring into the town to watch the filming and when I caught a glimpse of the Editor I fingered him a benediction to which he responded with a solemn bow. When the film came out, all the beauty and detail that had been poured into the camera from that day's work flashed by in a few seconds, the bulk of it having been thrown away, as so often happens with the movies. The whole operation would have been a sad waste of money had not the Journal photographer, Ken Upton, been there to record, with a marvellous series of black-and-white still photographs, how an old Cotswold town once went back in time to the days when it was young and new.

The only other time in my life when I got dressed up and stepped out in public ringing a handbell, was when I agreed to appear as Santa Claus at the annual Christmas matinée at The Playhouse Cinema at Moreton, at which a free film show for the children was followed by a distribution of gifts in the foyer. Their regular Santa was not available and I thought it would be a bit of a laugh to deputise for him though in the end the joke turned out to be on me. Of course, I would not have taken on the job had I not been able to disguise myself in the traditional garb. With that moustache and long white beard tickling my face and the red tunic covering my padded-out form, no-one would have known it was me unless he was told. Nevertheless, I must say that I felt nervous when the film show ended and the time came for me to make my grand entrance. Stepping out in front of one hundred and fifty children, ringing a big brass bell, is not the sort of thing you do every day of the week.

However, I stepped out, ringing the bell and shouting something appropriate, like "Merry Christmas, children!" and was given an enthusiastic welcome by one and all. Well, not quite all. As I walked up the gangway, I heard one of the older boys say, "He ain't Father Christmas! He's just someone dressed up!" As he was a boy, whom I had had to reprimand when I caught him damaging the pavilion of the tennis club, of which I was then secretary, I was tempted to turn round and say, "Yes, and wouldn't you get a hell of a shock if you knew who that 'someone' was!" but I desisted. All the same, I noticed that when the time came, the older boys did not hesitate to join in the queue for a free gift. I sat on a seat in the foyer by a Christmas tree and distributed the presents from a big sack. The older boys looked very sheepish and glanced at the smaller ones as if to say, "Don't get the idea we believe in this rubbish! We're playing along strictly for what we can get out of it!" It was the younger children whose behaviour took me so much by surprise and who turned what I had thought was going to be a joke into something quite heartrending. They really believed I was Santa Claus!

Some were so shy that they could scarcely force themselves to come near me or look in my face. They just grabbed their presents with trembling hands and hurried quickly away, but the majority wanted to talk and keep talking with me. When they discussed what they wanted for Christmas, it was not too difficult though I soon realised that I had to be very careful not to commit myself to promises that might never be kept. I groped for replies which could be taken in different ways. When a little boy asked me whether I could bring him a bicycle for Christmas, I told him, rather cleverly I thought, that this all depended on whether I could get it down the chimney, but he rather floored me by asking, "Why not leave it at the front door?" The really difficult part was when the children became personal. What could I say to the little girl who asked whether I could bring her daddy home for Christmas? I said I would try. Was that the right thing to say? The perspiration permeated my beard as I flushed at the thought of putting a foot wrong.

For the truth was that I had unexpectedly become not only the upholder of an ancient tradition – that of a kindly old gentleman who never disappoints little children – but also the custodian of a child's precious aspirations. It was a responsibility that I neither wished for nor enjoyed. The children seemed satisfied with my performance and whether I promised too much or too little is something I shall never know. All that I am sure of is that I would never want to be Santa Claus again.

CHAPTER ELEVEN

Parish Councils

I ONCE WROTE A parody of a parish council meeting though, in fact, it could have been a verbatim account of a good many actual meetings I attended. It went as follows:

Chairman:	What do you think, Fred?
Mr. A:	It needs doing.
Mr. B:	It's got very bad.
Chairman:	We want someone with a scythe.
Mr. A:	Or a gang mower.
Chairman:	You'd never get one of those in there.
Mrs. C:	I've got a lawn mower, if that's any good.
Mr. B:	No, it's too rough, Florrie. It's been let go.
Chairman:	Is there anyone who'd do it?
	Silence
Mr. A:	What about Bert Hoskins?
Chairman:	Which Hoskins is that then, Fred?
Mr. A:	Rectory Cottages.
Chairman:	Oh, Doll Tabor's son. Doll Tabor that was, I mean.
Mr. B:	I thought he lived down at the Mill.
Mr. A:	That's Ron.
Mr. B:	The one that had that motor cycle crash?
Mr. A:	Yes.
Chairman:	I thought he was on the building?
Mr. A:	Who, Ron?
Chairman:	No, Bert.
Mr. A:	He does a bit of part-time mowing.
Mr. D:	What about the Pasture ditch, Cyril?
Chairman:	Just a minute, Jack!
Mr. D:	It's got very bad.
Mrs. C:	You know why that is. People keep putting rubbish in it.
Chairman:	Just a minute! Let's get this other business sorted out first.
Mr. D:	What business?
Chairman:	The grass cutting.
Mr. D:	Oh!
Chairman:	Is anyone going to make a proposition?
	Silence
Mr. A:	I will if no-one else will.

Chairman:	Is there a seconder?
Mr. B:	Yes.
Clerk:	A seconder to what?
Chairman:	The motion.
Clerk:	What motion?
Chairman:	About getting the grass cut.
Clerk:	You can't. It's not our property.
Mr. A:	I beg to differ.
Clerk:	I tell you it's not our land!
Mr. A:	Before the First World War the parish council got Hacker Horton to go in there four times a year to cut the grass.
Clerk:	They never did!
Mr. A:	And I know they did!
Clerk:	That land in Wood Lane has never belonged to this council.
Chairman:	We weren't talking about Wood Lane. We were talking about the Plantation.
Clerk:	Well, why didn't you say so? The last I heard you were talking about Wood Lane. What did you decide about that?
Mr. A:	What did we decide, Cyril?
	Silence
Mrs. C:	I don't think we decided anything, did we?
Chairman:	Yes, we did! We're putting it on the agenda for the next meeting.
Mr. D:	It's in a terrible state!
Clerk:	What is?
Mr. D:	The Pasture ditch.
Clerk:	I thought you was on about the Plantation?
Chairman:	We was – were.
Clerk:	Well, what have you decided? It's got to be put in the minutes if expenditure is involved.
Chairman:	What do you think, Fred?
Mr. A:	It needs doing.
Mr. B:	It's got very bad.
Chairman:	We want someone with a scythe…

As the above may have revealed I had what you might call a love-hate relationship with parish councils. I loved them because they were my most dependable source of copy. When you have a large amount of space to fill each week it is no use leaving everything to chance. You have to be sure of a certain amount of good local material coming in to form the basis of the paper and this the parish councils never failed to provide. There was nothing more uplifting than to be at a meeting in a week when copy was running low and to hear a parish council launch off on another escapade that would land them in no end of trouble but provide us with some splendid copy. The parish councils' nerve and imagination never seemed to fail them and they would take on anybody from a Government minister to a Chief Constable or startle their own parishioners by attacking those who did not clean their windows, thus spoiling the appearance of the town, as happened at Campden, or introducing a "do-it-yourself" scheme to enable volunteers to do the council's manual work and thus reduce the parish rate, as happened at Moreton. They had no real power, no administrative clout, but they had a voice which they were never shy to use and whose utterances I was only too happy to record in the newspaper.

On the other hand, I hated (though that is putting it a bit strongly) parish councils because they simply would not get a move on at their meetings. After wasting the first hour, chewing over the minutes of the previous meeting, they would then waffle their way through the rest of the agenda with the clock advancing one, two, three, even four hours, by which time you would feel punchdrunk from words. Most parish council meetings could have been over in half the time but circumlocution and repetition were endemic to them all. Bourton-on-the-Water were the quickest but had a habit of going into committee more often than the others: either this or apparently declaring the meeting closed, knowing that Press and public would immediately stampede for the door, leaving them still sitting at the table and thus able to continue their meeting informally – and in private! At Stow, they all talked at the same time, while at Blockley they would get tantalisingly within an inch of home, then veer off into a discussion about something quite trivial, like the ownership of a ditch, and prolong the meeting interminably. Moreton had sub-committees but rarely used them with the result that matters that could and should have been delegated, had to be discussed by the full council, and Campden's meetings went on so long that they had to have two meetings a month instead of one like everyone else.

The trouble lay with the chairman. The Parish Councils' Association used to hold courses for parish clerks, the most efficient and conscientious performers at parish level, needing little guidance in what to do, when what they should have done was to organise courses for chairmen on how to conduct a meeting, something that few of them knew anything about. When a parish councillor was elected to the chair he seemed to regard this as some kind of recognition of his popularity rather than a duty imposed on him to see that meetings were conducted with order and dispatch. Obviously I, as an impatient onlooker, had a vested interest in wanting meetings to be over quickly, but it was repeatedly my experience that a meeting that dragged on accomplished less than one that was brisk and to the point, and that a council, who wasted too much time on the first half of their agenda, invariably had to scamper through the second half, giving less attention than they should have done to important new business.

Amendments were put to a meeting when they were clearly a direct negative to the original proposition and thus ineligible. When a chairman voted, he was said by his fellow councillors to be using his casting vote when he was doing nothing of the sort but merely using the vote he was entitled to like any other member. His casting vote was the second vote he kept up his sleeve to resolve deadlocks. The proper procedure for going into committee was never observed though, to be just, parish councils rarely turned out the Press. Because they trusted us, they would simply turn round and say, "Don't report this, please!" and carry on with us still there. And at the end of the meeting, the average parish council chairman would go on asking. "Any other business?" ad nauseam, when he should have sensed that the majority had had enough and politely closed the meeting, instead of throwing out further invitations to the odd man out, of which there was always one, who would go on talking all night if given the chance. If a chairman saw his colleagues stealthily creeping out, hats and coats in hand, he should have twigged that he was not doing his job properly – and that it was getting near closing time!

Parish councils were required by law to hold an annual parish meeting, open to all, at which to give an account of themselves and hear the electors' views. The statutory month used to be March but the period for the meeting was later extended to include April and May. On this glorious evening, the council would be pushed into the background and the people would take over who normally held their discussions in bars, at women's circles or privately over the family hearth. Little wonder that councillors blenched when Spring and the annual reckoning drew near, and many a parish clerk must have gulped on reading the minutes of the previous year's meeting to

Parish Councils

discover all the things the council had been asked to do and had subsequently left undone! Parish councils usually had a lot of explaining to do when confronted by the electorate en masse though, regrettably, many voters ignored this democratic opportunity to chide the council and put them right, and parish meetings were thinly attended except when a particular controversy, like the duck pond affair at Moreton, blew up. The riband went to Campden which always managed to muster a full house for the parish meeting no matter what the prevailing parochial temperature was.

An occupational hazard suffered by parish councils in the North Cotswolds was that of being locked out. None of the councils had their own meeting place, which meant they had to hire accommodation with the result that booking errors could occur. Bourton Parish Council once had to meet in a doctor's surgery when they could not get into their usual rendezvous, which was locked. Moreton Parish Council occasionally got locked out because the caretaker of the Congregational Hall forgot to unlock the door, and they also arrived at the building on one occasion to find the Horticultural Society in occupation, the building having been double booked. As usual, possession proved nine-tenths of the law and it was the horticulturists who remained and the councillors who had to withdraw. A similar misfortune befell Campden Parish Council whose proposed meeting place was occupied by a dramatic society in rehearsal. They, too, had to withdraw despite a call for the use of force from an ebullient ex-Army officer, who was then the council's chairman. When Blockley Parish Council were locked out of St George's Hall, the members had to scour the village for a key because the caretaker, who should have unlocked the door, was away on holiday. The most frustrating experience of all was at Stow when the agenda circulated to all members in advance said the meeting would be at half-past seven, which was a mistake because the council always met ar seven. When the night of the meeting came along, eight of the nine parish councillors turned up at seven, as usual, because they had not bothered to read their agendas, and had a chilly wait of half-an-hour because the building where they were due to meet stood locked till half-past seven. The missing ninth member was the only one who had read the agenda and he was the one with the key!

CHAPTER TWELVE

Obituaries

MY FATHER USED to tell me that when he was a young man, he had an old aunt who lived alone and was not often visited by her relatives, though they were all fond of her in their way. One day the family received a message that the aunt had died and was to be buried later that week. When my father and the other relatives arrived for the funeral, they were surprised to see the old aunt standing on the doorstep, as fit and cheerful as she had ever been, and inside the house, the table was loaded with good things to eat and drink. Asked for an explanation, she admitted that she had sent out the message that she was dead. "I knew you would all come to my funeral," she said, "but what good would that be to me then? I wanted to see you now." For the rest of the day, the family, dressed in mourning, enjoyed an hilarious party.

I often thought of this story when reporting funerals in the Cotswolds and hearing that a daughter had travelled all the way from Scotland or a son flown home from Australia in order to be present. What pleasure such visits would have given if they had taken place while the dead person was still alive and could enjoy the pleasure of his children's company! All of us mean to visit old friends or relatives but never find the time to do so, yet when we heard that one of them is dead, we move heaven and earth to attend the funeral. It seems as if we all respond to a deep-rooted urge to pay our last respects to the dead even though we may have been less than attentive towards them when they were alive.

This paying of respects is not as simple as it might appear, according to one or two elderly people I talked to on this subject in the Cotswolds. There is a proper ritual to be observed. Did you know, for example, that when the family mourners leave the house for the funeral, the front door should not be closed? It should either be left wide open or slightly ajar to avoid "shutting out the dead", which is deemed an act of disrespect. The woman who has laid out the remains has the right, if she chooses, to pour tea for the bereaved family after the funeral. She should arrive in good time, so that she can put on the kettle after the mourners have left for the church, her presence being useful because under no circumstances should the house be left empty. This is considered a serious breach of funeral etiquette. The undertaker can, if he wishes, arrange the mourners in what he considers to be their correct order of precedence, though he usually eschews the privilege nowadays. The important thing is that there should not be an odd number of mourners. All the family should leave together and not arrive at the church in ones and twos; and after the service, every relative should be asked to partake of refreshments, no matter how reproachful his or her conduct may have been in the past. If it can be avoided, the remains should not be allowed to "lie over Sunday" because this is believed to result in another death before the month is out. Or is it before the year is out? Whichever it is, it is best to get the funeral over before the week-end.

Once, I attended a funeral at Evenlode at which the usual ritual was abandoned. We were told the women should wear their brightest frocks, the bells were to be rung and cheerful hymns, sung. The idea was that the funeral should be a joyous thanksgiving for a happy life, now peacefully brought to a close. Of course, it did not work out like this at all. Everyone was trapped between forced smiles and unforced tears. There was also the funeral of a Moreton man who was a popular customer at the local pub. When his friends arrived at the funeral they were told to gather at the pub afterwards where it was announced that before he died, their old friend had arranged to stand them a last round of drinks after the funeral so that they could toast his memory and not be downcast and sad. But human nature being what it is, his wish was not fulfilled. When the company stood with raised glasses facing the empty chair in which their friend had so often sat and a toast was proposed to "our absent friend", there was scarcely a dry eye in the place!

I regarded the writing of obituaries as an important part of my work because it gave the paper an opportunity to show that it cared about its readers by giving a respectful mention to one of their number when he or she died, I remembered how we at home had treasured the yellowed cuttings of newspaper reports of loved ones who had died and been written up in the local paper for the first and last time. Not that the lives of ordinary people are necessarily lacking in interest. There always seemed to be something to write about, if

All Over the Wold

only the prolixity of their offspring, and surprising facts could sometimes emerge. Take Harry Gooding, of Stow, for example.

When I heard that he had died, I assumed that he was just another Cotswold craftsman, a slater by occupation, who had spent all his life in Stow, but his family soon corrected this impression, when I called on them, by telling me of an experience in his youth that few other Cotswold slaters could equal. It appeared that when Henry Ford, the American motor magnate, visited England in 1927, he was so impressed by the beauty of Cotswold architecture that he decided to build himself a house in similar style in the United States. He bought most of the materials in this country but when he returned home, could not find the right sort of craftsmen to carry out the work. So, after taking advice about the best man for the job, his agents asked ordinary Mr. Gooding whether he would cross the Atlantic to undertake the roofing of the house in true Cotswold fashion. He consented and spent several months working in America. The house was built at Detroit amid a great deal of publicity, and chippings from Mr. Gooding's stone slates were much in demand by souvenir hunters. While abroad, he was driven around by a chauffeur, who took him to see Niagara Falls, a far cry from the Cotswolds! Afterwards he returned to his former quiet life at Stow, building or repairing stone roofs, and was working on Barton-on-the-Heath church until only a few days before his death in December 1961.

Sometimes the circumstances of a death could be rather poignant. Samuel James and his younger brother, John, who were also natives of Stow, were inseparable. Their lives conformed to an almost identical pattern. They both worked as roadmen for the Gloucestershire County Council for most of their lives and when John married, Samuel made his home with his brother and wife, and they all grew old together. When Mrs. James died, the two brothers were left on their own, living quietly at King George's Field, looking after each other, their working days over. Then, John's health began to fail and at the age of seventy-five he was taken to hospital. Samuel, who was eighty, was taken to the same hospital soon afterwards: he, too, had grown tired and died late on Wednesday. The following Sunday morning, without ever knowing his brother had gone before him, John also died.

When the death of Major Lawrence Johnston occurred in the South of France in 1958, he left no relative living locally and I had to

Obituaries

turn to someone outside the family for help with compiling an obituary report. Though his last years were clouded by ill-health, Major Johnston was one of those few fortunate men to succeed in achieving their life's ambition. As a newcomer, aged thirty-six, he had stood in an obscure corner of the Cotswolds, and resolved that here he would create a noble garden, and when he died, fifty years' later, he had not only created his garden but had survived to hear it acknowledged as one of the finest in the country. The garden is at Hidcote Manor, where the Cotswold escarpment drops suddenly among a welter of trees, to Mickleton in the valley, and it has been described as a collection of cottage gardens. Going round, you certainly get the impression of walking from compartment to compartment, from one surprise to another.

When I heard that Major Johnston was dead I went over to Hidcote to talk to Edward Pearce, the only gardener who had been there from the beginning, to see what he could tell me about the man. An upright and active seventy-six, Mr. Pearce was weeding the potatoes on his allotment after a full day's work in the garden, when I called. "Major Johnston and his mother first came here in 1907, when Mr. Tucker gave up the farm that Michaelmas," he told me. "My brother and me were working at Mickleton and work got a bit scarce and the chap we worked for said we would have to go off for a few weeks. We was about here doing nothing and Major Johnston asked whether we would help him do his garden and we said, 'Yes.' That was a fortnight before Christmas and I have been here ever since, bar the war years when we was all on service. When I started with him I was twenty-six that same November and he was ten years' older than me. He wasn't a very large man: about medium build, I suppose you could call him. He was a decent sort of man and if you satisfied him he would pat you on the shoulder and say it was good, or if he saw anything special in the garden, like autumn colouring, which he thought was a lovely piece of work, he would come and fetch you to look at it. There was no garden then: only a bit of a vegetable garden where that cedar tree stands on the lawn. All what you see now he manoeuvred about, winter after winter, and fixed it up. There was a fair bit of hard work done about this place, I can tell you.

"He used to go abroad along with one or two of 'em and collect plants and seeds from different places and bring 'em back here, and he would order a smart few from abroad. That as came up to his

All Over the Wold

liking, he kept on with, and that as didn't, he threw away. Major Johnston was in the South of France for nine years or so before he died. He came back here once or twice to see the garden, and they tell me he often used to talk about it to his servants in France."

As I mentioned in the obituary, one of the last things Major Johnston did before going abroad for health reasons, was to give his garden to the National Trust to be preserved in perpetuity for the enjoyment of garden lovers. Now he is dead and lies buried at Mickleton but his monument lives and grows at Hidcote, two miles away on the hill.

The deceased in the Cotswolds could be ancient as well as modern because workmen were often turning up skeletons of our prehistoric forbears, especially in the vicinity of the Roman Fosse Way. Late one afternoon I received a telephone call from the then Rector of Stretton-on-Fosse telling me that a skeleton had been found in the village sand pits. The Coroner had given instructions for it to be re-interred and if I wanted to see it, I would have to get over there right away. As it was round about the shortest day of the year, it was already pitch dark when I reached the sandpits. At first I thought I had had a wasted journey, then I saw a light flashing inside a shed and went over and knocked on the door. Someone opened the door and flashed an electric torch in my face and after I had explained who I was and what I had come to see, a man's voice asked me to step inside. The torch then shone in the direction of a bucket on the floor which contained a human skull and bones.

A hand went into the torch beam, picked up the skull and thrust it into my hands. It was reddened by the sandy soil in which it had been buried for so long but was otherwise in perfect condition, the teeth being remarkably preserved. The man told me he had found the skeleton in a crouching position with its head between the knees, indicating, so he said, a pre-Roman burial. It had been only about eighteen inches below the surface of the ground when discovered. After I had asked him further questions, he took the skull from me and put it back in the bucket and I departed – without having the faintest idea of what the person I had been interviewing looked like! Because of the darkness all I ever saw of him was his hands!

A death that affected all of us was the assassination of President John Kennedy in November, 1963. That Friday evening, when the news began to come through to us in Britain, I was due to report on "Antigone", a doom-laden play in a doomed building, the Campden

Grammar School assembly hall, which was to be demolished immediately afterwards to make way for a new comprehensive school. I told the head master, Alan Jones, and the play's producer what had happened, when we met in the corridor, and they were anxious that the youthful cast should not hear of it until the play was over because it might upset them and they withheld the news till then.

The day after the assassination I had to cover another play, this time a comedy, "Who Goes There?", at Kemerton village hall, near Tewkesbury. I went to Evesham during the afternoon, as it was Saturday, to do some window shopping and have tea before going on to the play but felt utterly miserable and on the verge of weeping most of the time. The next day, Sunday, was no better. Some friends and I had been invited over to a house at Stratford for the day and four young children were there, Ann, Mark, Ian and Sharon, not that I could warm to their company with the mood I was in. After lunch, I sat in a corner away from the others with a Sunday paper in my hand and started to write a poem expressing what I felt, in the margin of the paper. While I was doing so, the news came through that the alleged assassin, Oswald, had himself been shot. When I had finished the poem, such as it was, I felt a completely different person, as if a weight had been lifted off my shoulders, since when I have greatly envied those people with genuine talent who are able to release their feelings in this way through their creative work. We took the children into the small public garden behind the Royal Shakespeare Theatre and played games with them among the golden leaves on the grass beside the river and had a wonderful time, romping in the autumn sunlight, and I had never felt happier in my life. The poem appeared in the next issue of the paper beside the Editor's leading article deploring the President's death.

> Here was a leader
> Who did not forget
> Those dreams men have
> When they are young
> To put the world to rights:
> He tried and left it
> Better than it was.
> Honour him now whom
> Unjust death has taken:
> Our world has lost a hero
> And a friend!

CHAPTER THIRTEEN

Linage

LINAGE IS THE means by which a reporter can supplement his income by selling stories to other papers, either provincial or, more lucratively, national. The name derives from the old custom of paying so much per line though this has been supplanted by a scale of payments, the size of which depends on how generous they are prepared to be and how much value they put on the particular story you send through. The Journal were prepared to turn a blind eye on linage provided you did not send material to papers with whom they were in competition or allow linage to take up so much of your time that you had none left for them. In any case, they benefited from the arrangement, too.

Apart from the obvious advantage of keeping their reporters happy, perk-wise, there was also the prestige element of their staff men being the official correspondents for the area rather than those of a rival newspaper; and sometimes, the first hint we had of a major local story came when a Fleet Street paper rang to ask us to do something for them about it, the story having broken at national rather than regional level. In particular, we were alerted in advance of local recipients in the New Year's or Birthday Honours by bigger papers calling on us on the eve of publication of the Lists to supply them discreetly with biographical details of the people in question to appear in the next morning's editions.

First, you had to get yourself accepted as the accredited correspondent for the town or area where you worked. When I moved into the North Cotswolds, I was the only reporter there and automatically became the correspondent for all the papers, daily and Sunday, and the BBC, though this proved a mixed blessing. It not only gave you the opportunity to earn money by sending stories to them, but it also gave them the right to telephone you, often at most unwelcome hours, to ask you to undertake inquiries for them. These could be embarrassing in the extreme, like going to ask the Hon. So-and-so, who lived in the Cotswolds but was not answering the telephone, whether it was true that he had broken off his engagement to his debutante fiancée. To refuse would have revealed to your high-powered Fleet Street caller that you had no stomach for the job and were unworthy of the name of Pressman; nor, as the recognised correspondent for his paper, was it possible for you to hang up on him as an ordinary member of the public could do. Prevarication was the only remedy and you could almost see the lips curling with scorn at the other end of the line as you tried to talk yourself out of a difficult assignment. And apart from the more sensational papers, there were also "The Times" and "Daily Telegraph" asking you to cover the funerals of local bigwigs, a task that meant standing in the cold outside a church door, taking down the names of the waves of mourners as they poured in for the obsequies. There was nothing more unnerving than trying to take down the rank and double-barrelled surname of some bowler-hatted military gent, and the Regimental Association that he represented, and seeing a backlog of serried mourners piling up behind him, waiting their turn to hiss their appellation and pedigree in your ear.

In fact, I often used to wonder whether linage was really worth it. If I stopped to 'phone through a story, it delayed the writing up of a report for the Journal, which had a knock-on effect on all the other routine jobs to be done that day, and there was always the possibility of the recipient of my copy ringing back to ask for further inquiries to be made, causing more delay. It would have been different if I had not been on my own and had someone to deputise for me, but this was not the case, and I eventually got to the stage of having to deny myself linage except when it could be managed without inconvenience, but, of course, major news stories never happen conveniently. To be marketable nationally, a story had to be sensational or somehow special and there were not many of these about in deepest Cotswold. It was demoralising when 'phoning through a story, which you thought was a good one, to hear a lugubrious copy taker at the other end say wearily, "Is there very much more of this, mate?" Nor did it help to have to introduce yourself as the correspondent for Moreton-in-Marsh, an announcement guaranteed to produce ill-concealed mirth in Fleet Street.

But even at my humble level, on the lowest rung of the journalistic ladder, the power of the Press was not to be sniffed at. When I attended a monthly meeting of the Campden branch of the Farmers'

Union, in the summer of 1953, there could not have been more than eight or nine members there. However, I managed to scrape together a respectable report because the speaker, Gerald Clifton, president of the Evesham and District Master Butchers' Association, had interesting things to say about the kind of meat housewives wanted nowadays. He said the customer liked smaller, good quality joints and unless the farmer could produce compact sheep and lambs, they were in real danger of losing their trade to New Zealand. It was a straight report of an obscure little meeting yet soon after it had appeared in the Journal, it was copied and splashed verbatim in the farming Press of New Zealand, half the world away, under the heading, "It's What British Housewives Want In Meat That Matters." How the report reached the Antipodes, I do not know though there were always unofficial linage vultures waiting to pounce on other reporters' morsels though, in all honesty, I would not have thought this particular one worth the pinching.

On another occasion a report of mine resulted in questions being asked in the House of Commons. This time I was both the originator of the report and the collector of the loot though it caused me no end of anxiety afterwards. It was in January, 1951, when the Labour Government was proposing to call up a body of men known as the Z-Reservists, because of the deteriorating international situation caused by the outbreak of the Korean War, and the plan was unpopular and under attack on all sides. At the height of the controversy, I heard that Moreton R.A.F. Station was to be closed and all the men sent home for at least three weeks because the camp had run out of fuel and could not be kept warm. The significance of this at a time when it was proposed to call up further men was obvious and I phoned a report to Fleet Street, who reacted excitedly and kept my 'phone busy for several hours. After their reports had appeared the next morning, a Member rose in the House of Commons later that day to ask whether the Government was still proposing to call up Z-Reservists when existing Servicemen were being sent home through lack of heating fuel. The reaction of an embarrassed Government was to order coal supplies to be rushed to Moreton R.A.F. Station and all the men's leave was cancelled. For weeks afterwards I hardly dared go out for fear of being set upon by angry airmen deprived of their unexpected leave!

It was also linage that led me into committing the worst howler a journalist can make, namely reporting an event that never took place.

Linage

It began when I wrote a long article about the Hoare family, of Chipping Norton, who rose early on the longest day of the year to watch the sun rise over the Rollright Stones, a prehistoric circle growing on top of a hill on the Warwickshire-Oxfordshire border like warts on the earth's skin. Legend has it that a witch turned a king and his knights and army into stone on this spot, and it is said that no matter how many times you walk round the circle counting the stones, you can never arrive at the same number twice. The Hoares had been walking to the Stones each Midsummer Day for as long as any of them could remember. They could not explain why they did so, only that it was a tradition the family had always kept.

My article was spotted by the News Editor of the "Birmingham Post", who telephoned to ask me to cover that year's walk for his paper. Unfortunately, the event fell on a Sunday and I was committed to spending that week-end with my father in Evesham. Not that I would have got up in the middle of the night to walk to the Rollright Stones with the Hoares: the "Birmingham Post" did not pay as generously as all that! As the Hoares were not on the telephone, I called on them during the week and again on the Saturday before leaving for Evesham and was assured that they would be making their annual midsummer pilgrimage as usual. I went to my father's as arranged, and telephoned my report, based largely on my earlier article for the Journal, to the "Birmingham Post" on the Sunday evening, having not the slightest doubt that the Hoares had kept their date with tradition that morning; but when I read the "Post" the next morning, I was horrified to find that my report had been replaced by another, stating that the family had not turned up at the Rollright Stones because they had all overslept! The Editor had sent a photographer all the way from Birmingham to take a picture of the family's vigil and he had been the only person there.

The following painful exchange of letters then took place between the News Editor of the "Birmingham Post" and myself.

Dear Mr. Day,
 I am sorry to say that I think you let us down very badly over the story of the dawn visit to the Rollright Stones to watch the sunrise. I sent a photographer and he was the only person there, as you will see from the cutting from this morning's 'Post' which I enclose.
 It is obvious from this, I am afraid, that you did not make any check on whether the usual visit had taken place. Moreover, the inaccurate story you did

send us was almost word for word the same as a cutting which appeared in the 'Evesham Journal" on June 26th, 1954. Had not the photographer been sent we should have carried a completely inaccurate story.

I have no doubt that this is a hardly annual to you, but even hardy annuals should be checked. I should be glad to hear if you have any explanation for what I think is a very bad let-down.

I would add that twice during the day we tried to get you on the telephone to let you know that the walk had not taken place, but were unable to reach you, but, naturally, we assumed that you would check. Under the circumstances, I do not propose to make you any payment for the story.

Yours faithfully,
L.B. Duckworth
News Editor

Dear Mr. Duckworth,

I can understand your annoyance but even after this space of time I do not see how the blunder could have been avoided. I must plead "not guilty" to being careless but "guilty" to being unlucky. I went over to see the Hoares twice and there was never any question of the walk not taking place: in fact, they wanted me to go with them.

I 'phoned through my report to you from Evesham and was unable to check whether the walk had taken place because none of the walkers is available by 'phone. I could have motor-cycled to Chipping Norton from Evesham but it would have been 46 miles there and back. I had already motor-cycled twice to Chipping Norton from Moreton, a total of 36 miles, and I could not imagine your wishing me to incur any more travelling expenses.

Besides, there was not the slightest doubt in my mind that the walk had taken place. It had not been missed for as long as anyone could remember. I might just as well have doubted that the sun itself had risen.

It is true that my report was taken from a report appearing in the "Journal" but having written an adequate report on that occasion, I could see no point in altering it to any great extent for your paper.

I apologise for the annoyance I caused you, though I must add that if my report had appeared no-one in the wide world would have known it was wrong except for the walkers, who would have been the last to speak. Facts are sacred but they can also be destructive. The highly accurate report you published has made the walkers a laughing stock and killed the old custom stone dead.

Yours faithfully,
D.B. Day

Linage

Dear Mr. Day,

Thank you for your letter giving your explanation about the Rollright Stones story. I agree that on reading it I think you were a bit unlucky, but if I may presume to give you the benefit of my own experience, I think the short answer to you is that if you are asked by anyone to cover a story, there is only one thing you can do – and that is to cover it – even if it meant going to Chipping Norton again, though I sympathise with you in this regard.

So far as "The Birmingham Post" is concerned, we place accuracy before everything else, including travelling expenses.

I am sorry the correct report we published has "made the walkers a laughing stock and killed the old custom stone dead", but really that is their fault and not ours.

Yours sincerely,
L.B. Duckworth
News Editor

CHAPTER FOURTEEN

The Smiths Move Out

IN JULY OF 1960 the Journal celebrated its centenary. There was a message of congratulation from the Queen, published in a 20-page souvenir supplement to which all the branch offices contributed a lengthy article, and a reception was held in Evesham's largest hall, attended by invited worthies of the Four Shires, as well as members of the Smith family, who had owned the paper from the beginning. One of them, our Mr. Raymond, a youthful-looking septuagenarian, was no less than the son of one of the founders, a whole century spanned by only two generations.

The Journal was then at its zenith as a family-owned paper. Its circulation was undiminished and it had never stood higher in public esteem. If people read something in the Journal they believed it to be true; and after years of being stodgily put together by whichever printer happened to be on duty at the stone, the slab on which the pages were assembled, the paper had begun to take on a more stylish, planned appearance, largely due to the influence of Bill Clarke, the reporter whom I had succeeded at Evesham during the war when he was called up into the Navy. Now a senior reporter at Evesham, he had explored the Journal's typeface resources and found riches, and with typical application had mastered the art of newspaper make-up in addition to his general reporting duties, and with the co-operation of the printers had begun to transform the look of the paper. Already it was moving towards the elimination of block capitals from headings in favour of upper and lower case, which provided an elegant uniformity, and the establishment of a centre spread, consisting of a letters page, faced by the "leader" and feature articles on exclusively local subjects. When the Editor, Mr. Monnington, retired, he was succeeded by Bill, an heir with strong local roots, generations deep.

Yet even in this bright centenary year there was a cloud on the horizon. The Smiths had no princeling to take over when the reign of the present generation ended. There were daughters but in those days there was little precedent for a woman running a newspaper nor, as far

The Smiths Move Out

as we knew, had any of the female line expressed a wish to take on this responsiblity. After a hundred years of success, the family had earned a celebration but it looked as though their days in the newspaper business were numbered.

By this time I had become the owner of a car. The motor cycle could not longer frustrate me by refusing to start or expose me to the excesses of wind and rain when transporting me on its back. Instead I had a 1935 Morris 8, costing £80, to take me about though before I could use it officially I had to learn how to drive and pass my test. To have a car and not be able to use it between lessons, except when someone could spare the time to accompany you, was frustrating and tempted me into going out on my own occasionally. When driving alone to Campden court, I had the experience of being waved down by a policeman who had recognised me and asked whether I would give him a lift to the court because his own car had broken down. During the journey he showed no sign of suspecting that he was in the hands of a learner, driving without L-plates, and himself the inadvertent aider and abetter of a misdemeanour!

When I took the test, the examiner proved to be a genial little man instead of the sarcastic, hostile presence I had feared, and he passed me first go; even so, my triumph was shortlived. The test caused me to be late for Stow court and when I arrived there, the word had already got around about why I was missing. "How did you get on?" asked the policeman on the door as I went in and my reply that I had passed was relayed to the rest of the court, which went on most of the morning. Afterwards, I got in my car, parked opposite the courthouse, and prepared to move off, the road behind being clear. A driver parked in front of me then got into his car and appeared to be going first, and so I gave way to him. As it happened, he was waiting for me to move and as soon as I realised this, I began to pull out. Alas! The road behind was no longer clear and I collided with a car that was in the act of overtaking me, the crash being witnessed by all the magistrates, court officials and police, pouring out the court opposite. It was the stuff that nightmares are made of!

Within a couple of hours of passing the test, I had been interviewed and cautioned by the policeman, who had welcomed me at the door, and issued with a notice of intended prosecution for dangerous, careless or inconsiderate driving. When I got home, I kept quiet about this and no-one could understand why I was so gloomy about having passed the driving test, something I had desired for months. If they only knew, I was half-wishing I had failed! After four weeks of suspense, I received a note from the police, saying that no proceedings were to be taken. Why I was spared when not even policemen escaped prosecution for driving offences, I never knew though I believe the man and woman in the other car were against the case coming to court for their own private reasons.

My father died on the last day of 1960, a victim, at least in part, of my zeal for the job. He had been suffering from bronchitis and as he lived alone, I had been staying with him at Evesham for the time being and commuting to and from the Cotswolds each day. The weather was cold and there was some ominous pre-Christmas snow about. The monthly meeting of Stow Parish Council fell on the Wednesday night and there was never any doubt in my mind that I should attend though it meant leaving my father on his own and staying overnight in the Cotswolds because of the snow, which was continuing to fall, making night travel hazardous. Ironically, when I got to Stow, I found that the meeting had been cancelled at the last minute to allow the council to go carol singing under the illuminated Christmas tree in The Square. On returning to Evesham, late the next morning, I found the house empty and a neighbour told me the doctor had called and an ambulance had taken my father to the hospital. He died of pneumonia ten days later at the age of seventy-six and it has since been greatly on my conscience that I ought not to have gone to Stow for the paper as I did.

By the mid-1960's, the introduction of improvement grants, by which an outright cash gift was made to home owners wishing to improve their property, was having a significant effect on the appearance of the Cotswolds. Houses were smartened up and derelict buildings rescued, including barns and stables that had outlived their usefulness and could be adapted into homes. Even a former pigsty was the subject of a planning application for conversion into a dwelling with grant aid! All the villages began to look better, some being transformed from architectural ugly ducklings into swans, and very little false prettifying went on. Enough masons and tilers, experienced in the Cotswold tradition, survived to see that the work was done well and the planners kept a sharp eye open for solecisms of design or detail. Some builders became so specialist in the conversion and improvement of old property that they did very little else.

The Smiths Move Out

All this enhancement of property resulted in towns and villages becoming far more sensitive about their appearance than they had been, and a yearly opportunity to see how they compared with their neighbours was provided by the Bledisloe Cup competition for the best kept village in Gloucestershire. This, the first such competition of its kind in the world, was started in the years between the two World Wars by Viscount Bledisloe, a Gloucestershire man and former Governor-General of New Zealand, whose name was commemorated by the cup he gave and whose latter-day kinsman, Earl Bathurst, president of the county branch of the Council for the Protection of Rural England, which ran the competition, presented the winner with the trophy each autumn. The cup almost always ended up in the North Cotswolds.

The presentation was one of the pleasant events of the year to report. Almost everyone from eight to eighty turned out for the ceremony, which took place out-of-doors on the village green, if there was one, and after some genial speech-making, Lord Bathurst would present the cup to the chairman of the parish council, a procedure repeated several times more till the photographers were satisfied with their pictures, then the corks would pop and glasses of champagne would be passed round for everyone to drink a toast to the village's success.

In the early days, the competition consisted of a straightforward choice of winner, then it began to get complicated. Instead of a single cup, there were two, one for the best small village, the other for the best large village or small town. This change was more or less forced on the organisers because the judges could hardly compare a village of 250 people with one with a population of 2,500, but it diminished the impact of the competition, and this process continued when a third cup was introduced for the best medium-sized village. Also, the organisers began to ask for hand-drawn maps and written reports of improvement projects, which made entering the competition more burdensome, and the judges sometimes made obscure or nit-picking comments, which parish councils, to whom their markings were sent, either could not understand or were irritated by. A number of councils protested at their meetings about petty criticism by judges, providing the Journal with provocative copy, and the Editor also had a go at the organisers in a leading article, accusing them of Philistinism in seeking tidiness from villages, where muck on the road meant farms at work, and weeds, a refuge for butterflies and other wild life. He went so far as to discuss with the staff the possibility of our running a rival competition with revised criteria.

The difficulty of choosing a winner was exemplified by the two parishes of Lower and Upper Slaughter which, despite their gruesome-sounding names, are among the prettiest in the Cotswolds though they could not be more different in appearance. Lower Slaughter has won the Bledisloe Cup on more than one occasion: Upper Slaughter, never, and looking at the two it is not hard to understand why. At Lower Slaughter, the brook, the houses and gardens are neat and delightful, a model of what an English village should be. At Upper Slaughter, the same brook is almost lost in a wilderness of weeds and the houses hide haphazardly in a green bower of leaves and grass. Probably more visitors go to Lower Slaughter and rightly so, because it is a gem of a place, but significantly, the film makers choose Upper Slaughter when they want to make a period picture of a village still in its "natural" state, as it might have been a hundred or two hundred years ago. Really there is nothing to choose between either village despite one being "tidier" than the other. They are both beautiful in their own way.

Improvement grants were also having a less desirable effect by reducing the numbers of houses available for local people. Outsiders found it a good investment to buy old properties and do them up as week-end or holiday homes and this involved knocking two or more cottages into one, causing a loss of smaller, cheaper houses. The Cotswolds were within easy driving distance of London and the roads were thick with traffic coming out into the country for the week-end on Fridays and going back on Sunday evenings. The trains were also full, especially the 17.15 out of Paddington, which would be packed with week-enders, many of them wealthy, whose drivers and expensive cars waited to collect them at Moreton, turning the station forecourt into a weekly miniature motor show. One week, this train of the elite broke down 200 yards short of the platform and knights, City financiers, company directors and past and present debutantes had to thread their way along the track, carrying their own luggage, while their chauffeurs stood baffled behind the station railings, unable to help them. Altogether sixty-three people had to complete their journey on foot.

When these modernised properties changed hands, they fetched prices far beyond the reach of local couples, who were obliged to move out of the Cotswolds if they wanted a home of their own. Private builders also seemed more interested in putting up expensive homes for retired people, attracted by the beauty of the region, than in providing the cheaper type of terrace house, which in truth is truer to the Cotswold tradition of high density than the detached mini-mansion and bungalow, and thus the housing problem, which had beset the district since the war, due to the shortage of houses, was now prolonged indefinitely by high prices as well. The social effects were rapidly felt. The average age of the district went up till no less than a third of the population of a choice place like Campden was aged sixty-five or over; village schools were closed because of a shortage of pupils, and shops that had once supplied the family went out of business and were snapped up by antique dealers as showrooms for tourist customers.

Not that housing alone was to blame for the drift away of the young. The Second World war and the years of compulsory National Service that followed it, had upset the old pattern of a man spending all his life in the district, where he was born. When I first became a reporter, I often interviewed people who had never been to London or the seaside and felt no particular wish to do so: the farthest they had been was to Stratford Mop, the ultimate excitement of their day. Conscription had changed all that. In 1955, for example, Moreton, with a population of less than 2,000, had its young men in uniform all over the world. Ken Hopla was sailing for Cyprus, Dickie Whitehouse had just returned from Ceylon, David Tarplett was in Jamaica and Jim Horne, in Kenya, Mickey Moulson was in Malaya, Denzil Harris, in Ireland, Ron Fowler in Ceylon, Bob Morgan, in Singapore, and George Baldwin, Les Newbould and Roy and Derek Walker, all in Germany. Obviously, the rising generation, which had the world as its parish, was not going to have the same outlook as its forbears and many were reluctant to stay at home when their Service days were over, knowing that jobs were more interesting and plentiful outside the Cotswolds.

Two years after its centenary, the Journal was put up for sale and bought by the old enemy, Berrow's Newspapers, of Worcester, owners of the less widely read Evesham Standard, which was extinguished after a while, their staff, our former rivals, being absorbed into our editorial department. It was a blow to those of us who disliked the

Berrow's formula of producing a dozen and a half papers each week, like sausages out of a machine, but we were told that no other offers had been received and that we, ourselves, must now become a part of that machine. Berrow's owned most of the papers in Worcestershire and Herefordshire and several others beyond, in places like Ludlow and Abergavenny, and it had been said that they flourished as a result of buying up the opposition. They certainly did so in the Journal's case.

Yet the effects of the take-over were by no means as unpleasant as had been expected. The new owners made it clear that they had no intention of interfering with the editorial side of the Journal, which they regarded as one of the jewels in their crown, nor did they; and our wage packets began to swell delightfully as the so-called house agreement and banding rates negotiated between Berrow's and the National Union of Journalists were applied to us, the newest employees of the group. My own income almost doubled in the space of three years. The N.U.J., which I joined, thereafter became a rumbustious presence in our lives, union membership having not arisen during the days of family ownership. If you wanted a wage increase or other entitlement, you simply collared one of the Smiths as he went about the building.

My only previous experience of a union came from covering the branch meetings of the National Farmers' Union, at which written resolutions were forwarded to the county branch and copies of the minutes were circulated to all members. Nothing was ever put down in writing at our N.U.J. meetings as far as I could see. Information was all by word of mouth, which meant there was little chance of checking whether it was true, and once the talking started and the meeting warmed up, all moderation usually went out of the window.

There was an occasion when it was put to us that we should withdraw our cars and make use of slower and less convenient public transport for getting to assignments until the firm was prepared to offer us better travelling expenses. Several members pointed out that when reporters on another local paper tried this tactic, they were more inconvenienced than the employers and lost the battle, and the whole tone of the discussion was that it would be an unwise procedure to follow, yet when a vote was taken, nearly all the hands went up in favour of withdrawing our cars, including those of the speakers who had argued most strongly against it. Eveyone wanted a fight and that was that! Working in a large rural area with scanty public transport, I had a miserable time in consequence. It took me two-and-a-half hours to get to Campden court, a nine-mile trip that normally took ten minutes, due to my having to catch a train to Evesham, then change to a bus to Campden, there being no direct service between Moreton and Campden. Fortunately, the action only lasted a few days because the firm caved in and gave us what we wanted. If the union's behaviour seemed odd at times, the employers' seemed even odder.

Not that you could fail to be stimulated by a union meeting. It was a wonderful feeling, especially for someone like myself, who worked alone, to find yourself part of a band of comrades, and there was no doubting the integrity and courage of the branch officers, who would bravely beard the bosses in their den with demands foisted on them by the meeting, no matter how preposterous these might be, and go back again if asked by the membership to do so. That they were prepared to risk present anger and future opprobrium from the management for the sake of the union filled me with admiration. I could not have done the same myself.

The truth was that I was not cut out to be a good union man. I was too much of an individualist to abide fully by the golden rule of solidarity. Though I wanted to do the right thing by my colleagues, I felt a greater loyalty towards the Cotswold readers and hated being involved in any form of disruption that would let them down. Relations between the readers and myself had become so personalised and interwoven that I found it impossible to say, "No, I can't help you this week because I've withdrawn my labour," to someone who had helped me the previous week. A one-man branch office, which depended so much on reciprocity of goodwill, could not operate like that. Also, while disruption might be all right in the Berrow's heartland, it was less acceptable in the outlying areas, like the Cotswolds, where competition from other papers was stronger. To win a concession from the firm by doing less or no work could prove a hollow victory with so much lost ground to be made up afterwards. All the same, I remained a member of the N.U.J. for ten years till walking out of a meeting of the Journal chapel in protest, never to return.

Soon after the war, the Journal introduced a pension scheme by which I would receive £7 a week on reaching the retirement age of sixty-five, a fair sum in those days when it equalled more than half my wages, but by the time I had turned forty, this sum had become patently inadequate and I badly wanted the N.U.J. to do something about it, but no-one seemed interested. The majority of members of the Berrow's branch were young birds of passage who simply wanted more in the wage packet and more time off and could not have cared less about pensions, with the result that I had to go on supporting actions for better pay, which I would gladly have done without for the sake of improved pension.

When a mandatory meeting of the Evesham chapel was called to discuss the terms of the latest Berrow's house agreement, which the union regarded as unsatisfactory and requiring industrial action if not improved, I asked whether it included a better pension scheme and when told it did not, I told them what they could do with their agreement and their union and went home in a huff. I must say that my colleagues on the Journal took my departure very well. There was no ostracism or unpleasantness though I got an admonitory letter from the Berrow's branch, telling me that I could not walk out of a union just like that, to which I replied with a formal letter of resignation. Working alone in the Cotswolds, I was beyond retaliation at personal level and too insignificant to be worth mounting a campaign about.

Although Berrow's were not prepared to be generous over pensions or the union to persuade them otherwise, they were much freer with their money generally than the Smiths had been. When life became intolerable in my office at the back of Lloyd's shoe shop, they bought new premises for me in Moreton High Street at what seemed an exorbitant price at the time though it proved a good investment. After his wife's death, Mr. Lloyd sold the shop to a man with a zest for do-it-yourself improvements and I worked amid the crash of falling partitions and the concomitant clouds of dust till I began to fear for my safety. One of the walls of my room was breached and had to be hung with tarpaulin to keep the weather out.

Having been unable to find anywhere to rent, I mentioned that an old, stone-built property, known as Fielding House, was on the market and to my surprise, Berrow's promptly bought it, something the family would never have done; and thus, at the age of forty, I found myself the tenant and de facto custodian of picturesque premises, consisting of two downstairs rooms, the front looking out on the trees and grass of the pleasant part of High Street, and the rear, on a pretty, enclosed courtyard, which I soon started calling the patio; and two upstairs rooms, potentially suitable for occupation. I had not only been provided with an office but a sequence of other rooms that could easily be adapted into rent and rate free accommodation for myself.

My old landlady, Mrs. Harvey, was now living in the first old people's flats to be built in the North Cotswolds, having been persuaded to move when her large, rickety old house became too much for her. By selling her house and moving, she had money in the bank and no more worry about repairs, an easily managed flat to run, no problems over heating, which was centrally provided, and a warden to lend a hand if she needed it, and she took on a new lease of life, surviving for another ten years, well into her eighties, yet to the last she maintained that she wished she had never moved and was back in her old home again.

The firm raised no objections to my using Fielding House as both an office and a home, an arrangement from which they benefited as much as I did because they not only had a resident caretaker but also an office manned 24 hours a day. The public quickly cottoned on to this and the telephone would start ringing soon after eight in the morning, or earlier if the caller belonged to a farming household, and continued till 11 o'clock at night, or later if it were the fire brigade or police informing me of a calamity. I had long since ceased to be regarded as a private individual by the majority of people, who simply looked upon me as the "Journal man", and by living over the office I became even more identified with the job. If ever a man was wedded to his work, I was, nor did I mind.

There was a minor drawback to living on High Street, however, which manifested itself within a week of my moving in. This man stepped in and wanted to sell me brushes. The next time it was a person selling office equipment, and from then onwards there was a procession of salesmen who, once they got their foot in the door, or to be more accurate, their tongues wagging, could not be dislodged or shut up. A gentleman with a long beard tried the same line of patter with me each time he called.

"Me holy man" he said. "You good man. I tell by your kind face. You have much luck. You have long life, many children… You want to buy shirt?" When I got a word in edgeways and told him that I did not want any shirts, ties or scarves, he gave me what I supposed to be his version of the Evil Eye and walked slowly and grandly out, as if gazing towards distant pagodas.

The only person from whom I bought anything was a woman with a North Country accent, who said she was selling soap in aid of the blind, though I had my doubts about her. She flashed what she said was an official hawker's licence in front of me but it went past so quickly that it might have been an old driving licence for all I could tell. I decided to give her the benefit of the doubt because blindness is such a terrible affliction that I could not bear to refuse what might be a genuine appeal.

"Ee!" she said, as she handed over two cartons of soap. " The folk in this town aren't half going to be clean by the time I've finished with them!" Clean, I wondered, or cleaned out?

Two years after taking over, Berrow's made a move that was to transform both the paper and the way we worked: they went over to front page news. Banished to an inside page were the classified advertisements, the smalls, which had adorned the front of the paper from the beginning and which were believed to be the fount of our prosperity, the magnet that drew readers to the paper. Now, more in keeping with the mood of the times, which regarded brightness of appearance as almost as important as content, news took precedence with a change of the front page and an inside page for each of our four editions, Evesham, Stratford, Tewkesbury and Cotswold. The Evesham edition presented no problems because there was a team of reporters at head office fully capable of providing enough hard news to make a good front page each week, but for those of us responsible for the other three editions, each a man working on his own, the innovation was far more demanding. "Have you got a lead yet?" became almost as much of a cliché as commenting on the weather when we of the Tewkesbury, Stratford and Cotswold branch offices were in touch with each other.

In order to be sure of a good front page I had to cast my reporting net wider, calling on people, visiting places and attending meetings not previously in my schedule until I was working most evenings as well as during the day. Even this wholesale commitment could not guarantee a lead for fifty-two weeks of the year, especially during August, the silly season, when everyone holidayed and nothing happened, and this was when ingenuity or even downright cunning had to be used. It was an exasperating feature of life in the Cotswolds that some weeks bulged with good stories while others had none. If I had more than I wanted and one of the stories would keep, I would sit on it till required though my hands would shake as I opened the opposition papers in case they had got wind of it too. At other times, when there was nothing in hand and no reserve in the larder and no amount of foraging could produce the goods, I would persuade friendly councillors to raise a controversial subject at their meetings, which I could then pounce on, and if all else failed and the occasion was public, I would get up and say something provocative myself, lighting the blue paper, as you might say, and retiring immediately, to sit down and hopefully report the consequent fireworks.

Some papers side-step the problem by elevating second-rate stories to the premier position and disguising the fact by sensational treatment, but the Editor, who was a bit of a perfectionist, insisted on a proper standard of front page story for the Journal. The lead had to deserve its position.

Berrow's next move was to begin the dismemberment of the Journal as a self-contained newspaper production unit by transferring the printing to their headquarters at Worcester, where all their other papers were produced. After the copy had been sub-edited, it was taken to Worcester for setting and an editorial team would go there every week to make up the pages on the eve of going to press, the Journal occupying a middle position in the queue of papers waiting to be printed. Thus, head office, itself, became a form of branch office. Copy was subbed there but the presses lay sixteen miles away and the old on-the-spot link between editorial and printers was severed.

Transferring the printing to Worcester may have made good economic sense but it was like losing an arm at the Journal and put tremendous power in the hands of the printers responsible for producing the entire chain of Berrow's papers, a power that they did not hesitate to use when they felt like it. The Journal failed to appear for two weeks during the spring of 1980 because of industrial action by the printers, a stoppage that Hitler's bombs and submarines completely failed to achieve during the war.

With the printing done at Worcester, the Journals were sent to the Cotswolds by rail on a Paddington-bound train, causing a manpower problem at their destination. When I moved to the Cotswolds, Moreton railway station had a staff of twenty; by the late 1960s there was a total of five, the only survivors of years of economising by

British Rail, and for much of the day there was only one porter on duty. After the booking clerk left at 3.30 p.m. he was in charge of the ticket office, too. The result was that some forbearance had to be shown by people using the station and passengers might even find themselves called on to lend a hand, as was the case when the Journals arrived . No one porter could have coped with this great load, which had to be got off the train as quickly as possible to avoid disrupting the timetable, and any passengers standing around would be roped in to lend their weight to the operation, a nice example of everyone pulling – or pushing – together.

As I sent all my copy to Evesham by train, I got to know the station well and frequently picked up stories there. Several of the staff were expert gardeners and won competitions for the best-kept station in the Western Region, their flower beds including a miniature topiary; and there was a fuss when British Rail demolished the up-platform's men's lavatory, regarded by some as a gem of Victorian ironwork. One evening, the 17.35 train from Worcester to Oxford forgot to stop and the dismayed Cotswold passengers had to be ferried back on a special diesel train, arriving home an hour later than expected. Almost the reverse situation happened when the 07.30 from Moreton to Oxford developed engine trouble immediately after leaving and took seventy minutes to do the seven mile journey to Kingham station. It never actually stopped nor did it get properly going, and the bemused staff at Moreton watched as it took a full twenty minutes to disappear from view. The blame was put on excessive frost that morning.

The highest point in the Paddington to Worcester line occurs a short distance from Moreton station. Beside the track lies a well, forming a source of the river Evenlode, and only a few yards away, on the same side of the track, springs a brooklet which runs down the hill into Knee Brook, a tributary of the River Stour. Let us now imagine that we are making a voyage from this point in a canoe we have brought specially for the purpose. At first the going is difficult but the infant Evenlode soon opens out and we observe how the railway follows the river all the way to Oxford, criss-crossing it over innumerable bridges. On reaching Oxford, city of dreaming spires and nightmarish traffic, the Evenlode joins the Thames and we are soon canoeing past such imposing monuments as Windsor Castle, Hampton Court and Battersea Power Station. Another bend in the river and we have reached the very Houses of Parliament,

The Smiths Move Out

magnificently a - bristle with gothic pinnacles.

In the Pool of London we exchange our canoe for a heavier craft for we are now bound for broader and less tranquil waters. After leaving the Thames estuary we proceed down the English Channel and soon, like all good patriots, we are standing wet-eyed as we watch England vanish into the mist. The Bay of Biscay gives us a stiff buffeting and we are relieved to reach the haven of Gibraltar. The skies are now a wondrous blue and the sun warms us as we traverse the length of the Mediterranean. After buying postcards from the Egyptians, we follow the Suez Canal into the Red Sea and shortly arrive in the glassy, heat-sick Indian Ocean.

Eastwards we steer till the exotic isles of Sumatra, Java and New Guinea are sighted but resisting the call of palm-shaded beaches and dusky maidens, we thrust on into the illimitable Pacific. An age seems to pass with nothing but empty sea around us and then, to our joy, the American shore heaves into view. We emerge from the Panama Canal into the Caribbean Sea, those doubloon-stained waters where many a sunken treasure ship lies, and bear northwards until the grey rollers of the Atlantic break across our bows. A boisterous ocean crossing brings old England into view once more, and we take course up the Bristol Channel, overtaking Lundy, the pirates' lair and the lesser isles of Steepholm and Flatholm. Up the Severn Estuary we go to where the lace-like tower of Gloucester Cathedral rises over the city rooftops. Our next call is at Tewkesbury, where we leave the Severn: for us the King John's Bridge is the first bridge over the Avon, not, as it is more popularly regarded, the last.

Our hearts beat faster as familiar landmarks rise around us – Bredon Hill and the Cotswold ridge, capped by the unmistakable Broadway Tower. The river takes us through Pershore and Evesham, with its green pleasure gardens, into the shallow reaches at Offenham and Bidford (We have now returned to our small, lightweight canoe.) Soon we are approaching the steepled church, where the greatest Englishman sleeps, but a mile or so before Stratford we branch from the Avon into its tributary, the Stour, which leads us through quiet Warwickshire villages to Shipston in the Vale of the Red Horse. At Tidmington, the Stour ceases to be a river and becomes Knee Brook, whose winding course we then follow into the Cotswolds to where it ends on a grassy railway bank, near Moreton-in-Marsh.

And here, after going right round the world without ever crossing land or going over the same stretch of water twice, we have reached the exact spot from which we started our voyage, the highest point in the main railway line from London to Worcester!

CHAPTER FIFTEEN

Capital Of The Cotswolds

THE COTSWOLDS WERE designated an Area of Outstanding Natural Beauty in 1966 to strengthen the hand of the planning authority in resisting unsightly development, though this did not prevent entrepreneurs from drilling for oil with Ministerial approval at Guiting Power and near Stow and Northleach. Whether the "Natural Beauty" designation would have protected the area from exploitation if oil had been found, which it was not, is a moot point. That they should have gone to the expense of drilling without hope of being able to profit from any discovery, seems unlikely.

Several years later the Cotswold Way was created, a long distance footpath, nearly one hundred miles long, from Campden in the north to the outskirts of Bath in the south, and this and the well-advertised charms of the area, swelled the already large number of visitors. Tourism was now the biggest industry after farming; the frugality of the post-war years had been forgotten and several of the Cotswold hotels were famous for their cuisine. At the other end of the gastronomic scale, hot dog vans drove into the district each evening to accommodate the late night trade by remaining open till the early hours, and the noise, smell and litter they created angered many of the inhabitants, who campaigned to have the vehicles banned.

A multitude of accents could be heard in Cotswold streets as people from all over the world began to discover the area, many of the visitors being Americans, who would call at my quaint looking office to introduce themselves, expecting to find, I suspect, a Benjamin Franklin kind of set-up with someone out front, wearing a green eye shade and trousers held up by braces, and out back, a veteran in an apron putting the type together by hand. Many were newspaper people who gave me their cards and told me to call on them should I ever be in their city.

As a consequence of the growing interest in the Cotswolds, a stream of guide books began to appear, copies of which were sent to the Journal for review. A number of the books were the work of rambling enthusiasts, who had compiled a selection of well-thought-out Cotswold walks, using the old network of footpaths, which went back to the days when the majority of country people had to walk to work, often over a considerable distance, and took to the fields if this were more direct than the road. Using paths for pleasure that were originally intended as a means of getting to work was not altogether fair on farmers, who would find a long derelict path across their land suddenly being used by scores of people as a result of it being mentioned in a book, or on the occupiers of houses, which had an old path going up their drives or through their gardens. When applying for a popular path to be diverted away from his home, the owner of Rissington Mill, near Bourton-on-the-Water, said that walkers were coming through his garden not by the hundred but by the thousand during the summer.

Yet the footpath books were a revelation as far as I was concerned. Before reviewing them, I thought I had better go on some of the walks described to test the books' reliability and found a world on my doorstep of which I had been sadly unaware till then. Each summer I had packed my bags and gone hiking in the wilder regions of Britain believing that this was where the real walking had to be done. Now, I found I could walk for hours through scenery as exciting, even as wild in places, as any I had seen elsewhere, all within a mile or two from home, and unlike being on holiday, when you have to take the weather as it comes, I could choose the right day for an outing. I got into the habit of going off most Sundays to discover the remoter parts of the Cotswolds: the lush trout streams fringed with kingcups and meadowsweet; the windy uplands, empty of all but sheep; the forestry plantations, with deep, steep valleys hiding old quarries, the haunt of moths and butterflies, and the unexpected vantage points from which could be seen the endless geometry of stone boundary walls, disturbed by the occasional crouching village or bristling beech clump.

I liked the autumn best when the bronze leaves of these same beech trees would mirror the sunlight, dazzling the eye with their colour, and if the world outside the office window was all aglow, I would sometimes sneak off for a walk, leaving such work as had to be done until the evening, and spend the next two hours roaming in the open air . It was on one such stolen walk on a Thursday afternoon, after we had gone to press, that I had an encounter with a stranger that had unexpected twist in its tail.

Capital Of The Cotswolds

I had been promising myself a five mile walk round the uplands above Northleach and after driving to the town and parking the car, I climbed up the hill to an old trackway, known as Helen's Ditch, turning now and then to admire the church tower, preening itself in the valley. All the expensive Cotswold towers seem to have been built to catch the light and pose glamorously like blonde film stars in a spotlight. After crossing the Fosse Way in a westerly direction, I found myself off course, a not unusual experience. Unfortunately, country footpaths do not behave in a logical way. They tend to veer off sideways into bushes or even temporarily double back on themselves: only the wrong paths go straight on and these were the ones I usually followed.

On this occasion, however, I was not to blame for being lost nor was my guide book, which I had brought with me and which told me to follow a track across the middle of a large field. The culprit was the farmer, who had ploughed up the track, leaving not a trace to be found. I did not feel up to blazing my own trail across the middle of this ploughed field, where the green shoots of the autumn sown corn were already appearing, even though I might have a legal right to do so. The farmer, if he saw me, might be carrying a shotgun. All I had to defend me was the guide book, which could possibly be wrong. So, I decided to walk round the edge of the field to see whether the vanished track would reappear in the next field, though this took me some distance out of my way. When I reached this second field, I was surprised to see the figures of a man and a dog against the sky ahead of me. When you get into the depths of the English countryside it is surprising how rarely you meet anyone.

One thing was certain. I was not on a recognised right-of-way and if it were a farmer, I might have some explaining to do. However, as he got nearer, the man, who was wearing a cap and old raincoat, did not look like a farmer, hostile or otherwise. He was more like a farm worker, though his casual pace suggested he was not then working. His dog was the first to spot me: a big black Labrador which romped over the field and sniffed round my legs before returning to its master.

We appeared to be miles from anywhere. There was not a roof or creature in sight: not even a cow, this being wide open arable country. When I got to the man he had his back to me and seemed startled, almost shocked, when I said, "Excuse me, can you tell me the way to Oxpens?"

He said, "You made me jump."

I replied, "I'm sorry. I've lost my way. According to this guide book there ought to be a track across that field but it isn't there."

"No," he said. "They've ploughed it up," then turning and waving his walking stick in the direction of a tree-fringed dip in the landscape, he added, "That's Oxpens, over there."

He was in his fifties and had a sunburnt face, bright eyes and a nice smile. He seemed a happy sort of man and I started to make conversation in the usual British way by discussing the weather. "It's a beautiful day, isn't it?" I said, gesturing towards a snaking belt of beech trees , aflame in the sun. "In fact, it's been a wonderful autumn."

"Yes," he said. "Me and the dog have been up here every day," adding, "Where are you making for?" I told him that after I had got to Oxpens, I intended to continue to Hampnett, then back round to Northleach.

"You'll be going that way then," he said, again pointing with his stick, and I could see a road on a hillside to the right, which was plainly the way I wanted to go. "Just follow the track to Oxpens, then bear right," he explained.

I thanked him and after wishing him a good afternoon, I continued on my way. I who had been lost, had now been put on the right path as a result of the directions given me by this helpful stranger, who had seemed so astonished to meet me. As I walked away, he called after me, "I'm sorry I didn't see you coming. You see, I'm blind!"

The local government changes of the early 1970s, which created new counties and merged existing councils into monster authorities, were as unpopular in the Cotswolds as everywhere else. There was a concensus that big was not necessarily beautiful, that larger councils meant larger wards and fewer councillors, and that local government was being unjustifiably de-localised. An absurd feature of reorganisation was that enviable salaries were offered to the officers of the new authorities, supposedly to attract the best talent from both inside and outside local government, but all that happened was that incumbent staffs applied for and were generally given the jobs and were thus paid considerably more for doing much the same as they had been doing before.

It was obvious that the North Cotswold District Council, whose presence at Moreton had been the main reason for the Journal having a branch office there, would have to go though there was a good deal of speculation about where to. The Journal hoped that the council would link up with Cheltenham District Council to cover the whole of North Gloucestershire, which roughly coincided with our circulation area in the county, and preliminary talks between the two councils took place to this effect. There was a good deal of logic to support such a merger. The people of the two districts were aware of each other as near neighbours, they went to the same places to shop, watched the same Midland television channels and were well-connected by public transport , but the North Cotswolds were scared off by plans for extensive industrial development near the motorway at Tewkesbury. The word "industry" did not ring sweetly in Cotswold ears unless prefixed by the soothing adjective of "light", and a further complication was that Northleach District Council, one of the weaker authorities, desperately wanted to tag along with the North Cotswold council, whose members, they rightly felt, were kindred spirits, and this made a northern grouping less tidy.

When Gloucestershire County Council, who had the biggest say over reorganisation, got down to discussing the matter, they lumped all the Cotswolds together from the outset and never gave the grouping another thought, though they wrangled long enough over what form the other five district authorities in the county should take. As far as they were concerned, the Cotswolds were one unit, even though the administrative area stretched a full forty miles from Warwickshire down to Wiltshire, was double the size of any of the other new Gloucestershire districts, and was thinly populated and unwieldy to manage. The five authorities to form the new Cotswold District Council were the North Cotswold, Northleach, Cirencester and Tetbury District Councils and Cirencester Urban Council and it was obvious that the admistrative centre would have to be at Cirencester, the only real town.

The grouping, which came into effect on April 1st , 1973, seemed at first to be a disaster both for the North Cotswolds and, less importantly, for the Journal. Each village had been used to having its own district councillor: now it had to share him or her with several other parishes. For example, one person had to represent the villages of Upper and Lower Slaughter, Upper and Lower Swell, Naunton, Guiting Power, Temple Guiting, Ford and Cutsdean, which had previously fielded seven members and together formed about a fifth of the North Cotswold council's total territory.

Candidates for the new authority had to be prepared to travel anything up to thirty-five miles across the roof of the wolds to get to Cirencester, which seemed as remote as Shangri-la, unconnected by public transport and accessible only by private car along the Fosse Way, thoughtfully provided by the Romans during their occupation nineteen centuries before. A number of potential candidates were discouraged from standing because of the travelling problem and the necessity to hold meetings during working hours. Evening meetings were out of the question because no-one wanted to drive by night over the high Cotswold in winter. To counter criticism of remoteness, the new council kept a branch office open at Moreton, where the public could seek advice from or have a showdown with a second eleven team of resident officers.

For the Journal, reorganisation meant that we had to deal with a council functioning in a town where no-one knew us, administering a district, two-thirds of which was outside our circulation area, yet we could not afford to ignore the new authority. All the important decisions about health, housing, planning and social problems involving the North Cotswolds would be made in Cirencester in future and we – or more precisely, I – had to be there to see that they were reported, though it meant a round trip of fifty miles a time from Moreton. Indeed, if the Journal had not been there our readers would have had very little information from an independent source about what was going on at the new council. The other reporters attending the meetings were all Cirencester-based and had no direct knowledge or experience of the preoccupations of the north, of which I was the sole Press representative.

As it happened, the shift of power to Cirencester worked out favourably for all concerned. If local government had to be reorganised and larger councils formed, it could not have been better done than it was in the Cotswolds. Though living far apart, the members found that they had much in common and evolved an independent collective mind of their own. As countrymen, they were conservative in outlook but fought the the Conservative Government tooth-and-nail over their decision to allow the sale of council houses, thus reducing the stock of houses to rent in an area where it was impossible for people of modest means to buy property because prices were so high. They represented a farming community but did not hesitate to castigate farmers over careless stubble burning and press for heavier penalties to be imposed on those causing damage and destruction.

They were a financially prudent council and unlike many of the other new authorities, did not immediately embark on building a local government palace for themselves but operated inconveniently for eight years from several different premises till buying an old building, the former Cirencester Workhouse, and rehabilitating it at very little cost to the public, as their headquarters, earning their reward when the Prince of Wales, one of their ratepayers, performed the opening ceremony and congratulated them on saving a characterful old building from dereliction. Above all, the council were determined that no part of their far-flung empire should feel neglected, particularly the north, which had suffered most, geographically speaking, from reorganisation.

As for myself, I was received so cordially at Cirencester – probably because the council appreciated my usefulness as a link with the north – that I soon felt as at home there as I had been with the old North Cotswold council, whose every meeting I had attended for twenty-five years; and if the Cirencester reporters from the Gloucestershire Echo, Swindon Evening Advertiser and Wilts. and Glos. Standard regarded me as an invader of their patch, they certainly never showed it and readily squeezed up the Press table to make room for me. I began to look forward to my weekly trips along the Fosse Way – not least because of the inflated travelling expenses they earned me!

Cirencester, itself, which the Romans called Corinium, proved a handsome town, eminently worthy of being the capital of the Cotswolds. Its picturesque narrow streets suddenly exploded into a wide central set-piece of church-dominated market place, enclosed by tall buildings harmonising well with each other, while just round the corner lay spacious, tranquil Abbey Park to which I would go to eat my sandwiches beside the lake during the council's lunch adjournments. There is a saying, "Scratch Gloucestershire and find Rome", and it is nowhere truer than at Cirencester, where the museum is full of splendid Roman relics dug up locally, while later ages have also left their legacy in the form of fine and varied architecture, all built of Cotswold stone. It was fitting that a place that was once a provincial capital of Roman Britain should have taken on a similar

All Over the Wold

sort of role again.

When the North Cotswolds joined Cirencester, I ceased to attend the meetings of Cheltenham District Council, who threw in their lot with the new Tewkesbury council, forming a body whose activities were more appropriately covered from our branch office at Tewkesbury. Despite its name, the Cheltenham council had not been responsible for running the Regency town, which had its own borough council, but the rural area surrounding it , much of which was Cotswold: hence my presence at their meetings.

I used to like going to Cheltenham because after the council I could stroll along the town's main street, the Promenade, with its leafy Parisian elegance, and wander round the shops, as good as any outside London. The snag was that in those early days I would frequently emerge from the meetings burdened with an acute sense of inferiority, the cause of which was my having to sit next to the Gloucestershire Echo's representative, Frank Browning, who was quite simply the best reporter I have ever known.

He was in his forties then, a shortish, wiry man with sharp blue eyes, modest moustache and face tanned from the hours he spent at his favourite pastime, playing golf. His thinning, straight brown hair was brushed flat but there was always a strand or two sticking up, giving him a slightly raffish look. What made him so daunting was his high voltage performance once a meeting started: it was as if someone had plugged him into the mains. He would take down a full note in rapid, immaculate shorthand, then as councillors waffled or repeated themselves, as they always do, he would snatch a wad of copy paper and proceed to write up the meeting in longhand, deftly switching from note-taking to reporting, as circumstances required, and refuelling himself with an occasional pull on his cigarette. When he had nothing worth taking down or writing up, he would collapse downwards on the table with his head buried in his arms, quite relaxed and inert, except for that odd quiff of hair still sticking up, then when the council had moved on to a more interesting topic, he would instantly crackle into action again. At the end of the meeting, as I was anxiously going through my notebook to see whether I had got everything down, I would hear him say, "That's that little job done, then!" and turn to see him patting his completed copy into a neat parcel, the entire meeting written up as soon as it had ended, in a brisk, lucid style that would need little subbing and could be sent to the comps as it was. The councillors and staff respected him as much as I did and would come over to chat with him during the tea break, totally ignoring me, whom they no doubt regarded as a presumptuous puppy to be sitting at the master's table, and this did not help my morale either. I used to think that Frank, the perfect reporting machine, would go off "pop!" one day, but I was wrong: he survived to enjoy a happy retirement and a well-deserved mention in the Queen's Honours List for his services to journalism.

Cheltenham District Council were the most itinerant of all the local authorities, whose meetings I covered. They had offices in one of the beautiful Regency terraces in Imperial Square, but there was no room big enough for the full council to meet there and they had to rent a council chamber for their monthly meetings. Immediately after the Second World War they gathered in a humble wooden shed at the back of Cheltenham Town Hall, an Edwardian architectural belch in the middle of the Square; then as their fortunes improved, they moved into the actual hall, using the magnificent Pillar Room, rich in marble and gold framed paintings, including one of a boatload of men desperately hauling for the shore, with whom I used to identify during long and boisterous meetings.

The Cheltenham council must have been the only one in the world to debate to the accompaniment of the Halle Orchestra, conducted by Barbirolli, which would happen during the annual Cheltenham Festival of Music, with the orchestra rehearsing in the main hall while the council held forth in the Pillar Room nearby. They were not always able to get the hall, especially during the festival, and would have to go on their travels: to the insignificance of the Old Town Hall, tucked away in a side street; the splendour of Cheltenham Borough Council's chamber, which looked like the inside of an opera house, or to the animation of one of the town's most popular restaurants, whose upper floor they hired. By 1969, the council had acquired the house next door to their offices and were able to reconstruct the two buildings to include a council chamber, thus putting an end to their wanderings, at least till re-organisation came along.

It was at a meeting in this new council chamber during the summer of that same year that a fellow reporter, who removed his jacket on a warm afternoon, was rebuked by a veteran councillor for his bad manners. It was true that everyone else, including me, was jacketed, despite the hot weather, reinforced by the central heating, but the reporter, who came from New Zealand, where they were probably not so particular about etiquette, could not understand what all the fuss was about. Nor could I, really, because the woman councillors had sensibly turned up in light sleeveless frocks with low-cut necklines, and no-one accused them of discourtesy despite their revealing far more than a man in his shirt sleeves would do. Our indignant councillor might have done better to insist on equal rights for men, but it was not until several years' later that the chairman of councils or magistrates' courts got into the habit of inviting perspiring males to remove their jackets in hot weather if they wanted.

A matter of dress also involved me in an embarrassing situation at a subsequent meeting of the council. I had noticed when driving into Cheltenham on a previous occasion that an enterprising farmer had installed a self-service manure stall outside his farm: you simply helped yourself to one of the full sacks he had stacked on the roadside and put the required sum in a collection box. Having decided to pick up a sack on my way in - thinking that I might be in too much of a hurry on the way back if the meeting went on a long time – I stopped my car by the stall and bent down to lift a sack into the boot, only to hear a terrific tearing sound below. The strain of my stooping and lifting had split my trousers from the waistband to the crutch! I had no time to go back home for another pair nor the means to do repairs on the spot and had to continue to Cheltenham with the sack of manure safely in the boot but the seat of my trousers flapping wide open. After parking the car fairly near the offices. I got inside the building as quickly as possible and sidled up the stairs with my back to the wall, following the same procedure in the council chamber before making a last quick dash from the wall to the Press table. The same tactic had to be repeated when I left and must have been successful because no-one commented about the trousers, which was probably just as well. Taking off your jacket seemed a minor solecism compared with appearing at a council meeting with the seat of your trousers gaping open!

I never asked Frank Browning about how he started in journalism though I have no doubt that like me he came of the old school which had no formal training and just learnt as it went along. A different school was now emerging of young reporters who had been formally trained and had a piece of paper, in the form of a proficiency certificate, to prove it. A compulsory national training scheme for journalists came into force in 1952, giving youngsters the choice of a one-year pre-entry course at a training centre, followed by apprenticeship with a paper; or direct entry with an immediate apprenticeship interrupted by two eight-week block release courses, roughly a year apart. Before recruits could qualify for the final proficiency test, they already had to have passed preliminary examinations in law, public administration and newspaper practice, and to have reached a shorthand speed of one hundred words a minute. It was a far cry from the old days when a paper would look for a likely lad from the elementary school, who had taken no examinations at all, and mould him into their own image.

After twenty years, the training scheme was having a significant effect on provincial weekly newspapers. Virtually all the training was done in the provinces and hardly a week went by without the Editor receiving an application from a would-be trainee, often boasting impressive academic qualifications. Openings on papers were few and applicants many, especially for a place on a paper like the Journal, which had a good reputation, but few of the trainees regarded their stint on a weekly as anything other than a stepping stone. The Journal saw a succession of youngsters from all over the country who, having completed their apprenticeship then flew on as fully-fledged reporters to a higher and more lucrative perch in the profession.

Instead of having an exclusively local recruitment, weekly papers were attracting outsiders without any real commitment to the area, which was usually unknown to them before their arrival. When local boys were recruited, they did not just want to be a reporter. They wanted to be a reporter for their local newspaper, serving a community whose character and traditions they understood. They lived at home, using an established network of relatives and friends as a means of gathering news , and with the possiblity of their marrying a local girl in a year or two, they were a much better long-term investment for a paper. (An incidental reason why the new generation of reporters failed to take root was that finding somewhere to live was not easy in a small town. Going into digs no longer appealed and flats were hard to come by and expensive to rent. The temptation was strong to move on when their apprentice days were over.)

The new boys also had a more hard-headed attitude towards the job. They were less inclined to regard it as a vocation, where the money was of a secondary importance, or to let it intrude on their private life. They certainly did not intend to be taken advantage of as we veterans had allowed ourselves to be through a mixture of apathy and loyalty to the job. We would look up with surprise as they rose and left at knocking-off time, which did not always coincide with the end of the proceedings in hand: surprised, not because they wanted to go home, which was natural enough, but because they did not appear to be curious about what the result would be of the particular court case, debate or whatever it was they were reporting.

As time went by, an ominous gap began to appear in the age structure of provincial editorial departments, including our own. There was an abundance of juniors under the age of twenty-five, doing their training before moving on, and of veterans of the pre-training days, aged fifty and over, sticking to the only job they had ever known, but few in their thirties and early forties "coming on" to take over when the veterans retired or expired. All the signs were that the day was coming when weekly newspapers would be staffed entirely by transitory young reporters from outside the area and that a significant local dimension would be lost from provincial papers.

My first car, the treasured 1935 Morris, was taken from me when a tractor driver turned right while I was overtaking him, causing me to swerve into a ditch from which I emerged unscathed but the car, a complete write-off, did not. After several goes with secondhand cars, which behaved badly, I took the financial plunge and bought a new car to achieve trouble-free motoring, and from then on I changed my car for a new one every two years and breakdowns became a rarity. Indeed, only two happened that left me stranded at the roadside.

On the first occasion, conditions were ideal for a disaster to happen. It was dark, late at night, cold, windy and pouring with rain and the car was crossing one of the loneliest parts of the Cotswolds as I returned from covering a first night at the Everyman Theatre at Cheltenham. Suddenly the accelerator pedal disappeared into the floor and ceased to function; the engine cut out and the car drifted to a halt on the side of the road. There wasn't a sound to be heard apart from the rain and wind beating on the roof. This could not be happening to me, I thought. My car was almost brand new and had only 1,000 miles on the clock yet when I switched on the car light and examined the accelerator pedal I could see something had gone very wrong with it. I stepped out into the rain and lifted up the car bonnet but recoiled at what I saw. There was not a hope of sorting my way through that awesome maze of wires and plugs. Obviously I had to get help but from where? I looked at my wristwatch and saw with misgiving it was nearly eleven o'clock.

There is something dreadfully final and hopeless about your car breaking down late at night, far from anywhere. The machine age with all its comforts and assurances, suddenly deserts you and you are like primitive man again, alone in the wilderness. Where was the nearest telephone? Who could I ring up if I found one? What would I say at that late hour? How could I get home to Moreton, fifteen miles away with no buses operating? There was a gleam of hope, however. About half-a-mile back there had been a small garage, the only building for miles. Perhaps its occupants were still up and could help me. I walked back along the road and my spirits rose as I saw a light still shining in the garage window. My knocking caused the inevitable dog to bark and eventually a man came to the door. I told him what my difficulty was but he said he could not help me. When I asked whether he was on the telephone, he said he was but refused to let me make a call from the premises. "It's not our policy to allow strangers in after dark," he said.

"What am I going to do then?" I asked, suppressing an impulse to burst in by force.

"There's a call box in the village, three miles down the road," he said. "That's the nearest telephone there is," and he shut the door.

So there I was, on my own again, three miles, apparently, from a telephone. As I was already half-a-mile's walk from the car, there seemed no point in going back to it, and so I continued walking towards the village. Overhead a leering moon dodged in and out of black clouds while the rain showered down. Why on earth, I asked myself, had I put on my best suit that evening when it had been quite unnecessary? I had never bothered to wear it to the Everyman before. And why, come to that, had I not thrown my mackintosh in the back of the car?

The road to the village went down an interminable hill. One or two cars went past but I did not try to thumb a lift. Who was going to pick up a stranger in a lonely place at that time of night, especially someone so fiendish-looking as to be refused admission to his premises by a garage owner? Then I saw headlights behind me and a sports car swerved to a stop some yards in front of me. As I reached it, the driver, a man, lowered the window and said, "I didn't see you in that dark suit. Do you realise I nearly hit you?"

I replied, "The way I'm feeling at the moment, I wouldn't have cared if you had!"

He asked what the trouble was and when I explained, offered to give me a lift into the village where, he said, there was an all-night garage, an unexpected though fortuitous amenity, I thought, for such a small place. When he asked what was wrong with the car, I told him and he smiled, rather patronisingly, I suspected. "Oh, that's easy, " he said. "very easy. You could have put that right yourself. It's only the cable needs fixing. Nothing at all really."

When he dropped me in the village, outside the garage, I thanked him and said I hoped someone would do the same for him one day though on reflection, I realised he was probably the sort of mechanically-minded person who would not need help anyway.

Inside a lighted cabin in the garage forecourt, I encountered the all-night staff, two of the plumpest, jolliest men I have ever met. I could hardly believe that people still up and working at that time of night – it was then about half-past eleven – could be so cheerful. When I sought their help, they seemed delighted to turn out in the rain to fetch my car with their breakdown van. First I had to assure them, though, that the car was not more than four miles away. "We can't send the truck too far because it's got a cracked radiator," they explained with a laugh.

With myself in the front seat, next to the driver, the van set off up the road with a roar, the raindrops dancing white like snow in its fierce headlights. As the vehicle vibrated its way slowly up the hill, the thought crossed my mind that it, too, might break down and then where would we be? But no such thought seemed to occur to the driver who was chatting about how he had skidded into a ditch, near Tewkesbury, the previous day. We eventually surfaced on the flat upland and shortly afterwards arrived at my car. After the driver had fastened a tow rope to my front bumper, I got into the car, ready to steer it the three-and-a-half miles back to the garage. "Now whatever you do, don't let the rope go slack!" he warned me before getting into the cab and driving off.

His warning proved impossible to obey. Peering through the streaming windscreen, I could see my car gaining on the van, with the result that the rope kept going slack. When it tightened, the car was pulled forward with a tremendous jerk, which left me trembling for the safety of the front bumper. As there seemed to be no alternative, I put on the brake and kept it on. Some distance further on, the breakdown van slowed to a stop and the driver walked back to me.

"Now what's up?" he said.

"Nothing," I replied.

"There must be," he said. "I can hardly pull you. You haven't got the brake on, have you?"

"As a matter of fact, I have," I said diffidently.

"You mustn't keep it on all the time!" he protested. "Just touch it if you see the rope slackening, then take your foot off again."

"But what happens when we go down that hill?"

"It'll be all right," he said. "You'll see."

It was all right, except when we went round that sharp bend and my car swung over to the opposite side of the road like a yo-yo on the end of a string. At least there were no more jerks and when we arrived at the garage forecourt, shortly before midnight, my front bumper was still in one piece. The driver was the first to look under the bonnet for the cause of the trouble and when he raised his head, all wet from the rain, he was smiling slyly. "This is going to make you laugh" he said. " This is really going to make you laugh! Do you know how long this job is going to take me? Three minutes!"

Half-an-hour later, the two of us were groping around the bottom of the car for a vital nut which had dropped out while he was re-inserting the accelerator cable. It was not really his fault. The nut had been put in such an awkward position that it was extremely difficult to remove and put back again. There was nothing wrong with the cable, he explained. It had not been properly connected in the first place. It should have been threaded through a hole under the dash board but had been resting in a slot above it.

When the nut had been found and the job finished, he told me to go into the cabin and ask the other man what the "damage" was. The "damage" proved to be much less costly than I had expected and after paying, I thanked both men and wished them a good night. They were settling down in their cabin again, wetter than they had been before I came but still cheerful. At no time during the hour that I had spent with them had they given the impression that I was unwelcome or a nuisance. Despite the time of night and the appalling weather, they seemed irrepressibly happy in their work and only too eager to please.

How many of them are there left?

On the second occasion when my car broke down, conditions could not have been better and it proved an idyll of a breakdown, not a nightmare at all. To begin with, I was not in a hurry. I was just ambling over to Campden with all the time in the world at my disposal, and it wasn't at night. It was mid-afternoon and instead of raining, the weather was bright and sunny with lumpish white clouds rolling across an impeccably blue sky. As the car was climbing the hill towards Broad Campden, the engine gently died away and the car slid peacefully to rest beside the grass verge. With the engine gone, you could hear the birds singing. I lifted the bonnet, then closed it quickly again after seeing that complexity of wires and plugs, each with a function unknown to me. All that I could be sure of was that I had not run out of petrol.

It was going to mean a walk again but who cared? It was such a lovely afternoon. People ought not be cooped up in a car on a day like this, I thought, and I set off in good spirits. The nearest garage was two or three miles away but it hardly seemed to matter. I picked a blade of grass and chewed it as I strode along, enjoying the visual banquet of verge and hedgerow, now in the fulness of high summer. Normally I would have been in too much of a hurry to notice. From the top of the hill, I could see the roofs of Broad Campden below and thought that I would try telephoning from one of the first houses I came to. This proved unnecessary because when I reached the village, a Midland Red bus was waiting , just like a taxi. Considering that there were only about two buses a day from Broad Campden, you have got to admit that this was a bit lucky, but that is the way this breakdown proved to be.

After I had got on board, the bus moved off immediately. "You're lucky," the driver said. "I'm a few minutes late starting today. Normally you would have missed me." I was not surprised by what he told me. I knew that everything was going my was that afternoon. As we travelled into Campden with myself the only passenger , I explained what had happened and he obligingly dropped me off at the first garage.

There, the mechanic was equally obliging. "Right!" he said. "We'll take a look at it right away," and after flinging his tools into the back of the breakdown van, he drove off with me in the passenger seat. Unlike the previous occasion, when the breakdown van, itself, showed every sign of breaking down, this vehicle gave no cause for alarm and we soon reached my car, still comfortably tucked into the side of the road. The mechanic asked me to lift up the bonnet, which I did, and without taking a tool out of the van, he gave a fierce thump on a certain part of the car's anatomy. The result was the engine was immediately restored to healthy, throbbing vitality! Oh, to know where to thump – and when!

I resumed the journey only half-an-hour later than I would have done if the car had not broken down. On reaching my destination the person I had called to see said, "I've just made some iced coffee. Would you like some?" Would I! And to think that if I had arrived half-an-hour earlier, there wouldn't have been any for me to have!

CHAPTER SIXTEEN

The Giants Move In

WHEN I BECAME the Journal's man at Moreton-in-Marsh at the age of twenty-one, I knew at once that this was the job I wanted to do and the place where I wanted to live, and nothing happened during the next thirty years to cause me to think otherwise. I hoped that I would be able to go on working for the paper in the Cotswolds till I reached retirement age and then go on working for them part-time till I dropped, if they still wanted me, but this was not the way it turned out to be. By the time I was fifty-seven, I was no longer with the Journal, with whom I had worked for forty-one years, or in the Cotswolds, where I had lived for thirty-six years, and if this book has any sort of moral, it is that things never stay the same and when they change, they do not usually change for the better.

Just as Berrow's Newspapers bought and swallowed up the Journal, so they in turn were bought up and swallowed up by the News Of The World, the national Sunday paper belonging to the Carr family, providing the Journal with an unexpected bedfellow. Then, they in turn were swallowed up by News International, the Australian Rupert Murdoch's organisation, which owned many papers, including the national daily, the Sun, another unexpected partner. Management became more remote; I became a number, 05/04360, in someone's large ledger and my office, an imperceptible dot on the vast News International map. As my wages were now sent by post, I had no occasion to go to Evesham unless asked by the Editor to do so nor did I want to. The staff had changed so much over the years that I felt like a stranger there and was glad to return to my Cotswold retreat as quickly as possible.

The Editor still decided what went in the paper and remained the centre of my world. He was only the local summit, however. Beyond him lay the Worcester range and beyond them, the distant peaks of News International, including Mount Murdoch itself. Everyone, except the man at the top, was over-shadowed by someone else and could have his modus operandi affected by decisions taken further up the line. In particular, the Journal was prone to price increases imposed from above, which put us at a disadvantage compared with other weekly papers in the area. In the Cotswolds, for example, the Oxford Times, Banbury Guardian and Wilts. and Glos. Standard had more pages than the Journal and generally carried a higher proportion of news to advertisements yet cost several pence less than we did, making life difficult for a district man, who somehow had to prove that his paper was worth paying extra for.

As I sweated to provide juicier copy, I was baffled why we should have to charge more when Berrow's had this ideal set-up of numerous papers mass produced from a centralised printing works. Even greater efficiency might have been expected when they went over to computerised offset printing in 1975 but we continued to be in the vanguard price-wise, alas! On the credit side, the quality of reproduction of our pictures was much improved by the new process; on the debit side, the transfer from hot metal to offset led to a horrible rash of printing errors. An article on the Cotswold front page was reduced to such gibberish that it had to be corrected and published again in full the following week before anyone could understand it. The rash subsided in time but inexplicable errors, often exquisitely painful to the author of the report in which they appeared, continued to plague us as never before. Nor did it help after seeing a report marred by a misprint to have the error laughingly pointed out to you by every joker you subsequently met. A diarist in "The Times" had fun at my expense when a report that I wrote about revised sittings for Stow Magistrates Court just would not come out right at either the first or second attempt and was spotted by him, though his teasing succumbed to a printing error itself in due course, which served him right! The Journal was by no means the only sufferer, as was evident from the growing number of magazines offering prizes to readers sending in the funniest misprints.

It was offset, of course, that opened the door to the free sheets. This process was so cost and labour effective that a handful of people could produce such a sheet, then distribute it free of charge on the strength of the income from advertisements. Their rates undercut those of established, traditional papers, whose operating costs were higher, and in common with other provincial papers, the Journal found its popular classified advertisements being siphoned off by the upstarts, and as they prospered, the free sheets included more and more non-advertising material, which could hardly be described as news but gave them the spurious look of a tabloid newspaper. They were more of a nuisance than a menace to a good paper though the inroads they made on local advertising were not to be taken lightly or their potential appeal to readers who simply wanted something to look at on a Friday without being choosy about content. The advent of the free sheets certainly complicated the local newspaper scene. It was no longer just the good old weekly rag being pushed through the letterbox every week.

Nor was I now the only reporter in the North Cotswolds, where I had reigned alone for the first thirty years. Other papers had moved men there, too, making it less easy though not impossible, to find exclusive material for the front page. Although I enjoyed having comrades-in-arms, especially during long meetings when we could joke or gossip our boredom away, there was an aspect of their presence that began increasingly to worry me. In the old days, when I had sat alone at the edge of a meeting in some chilly schoolroom or village hall, taking it all down in my notebook, it had seemed a natural thing to do; when there were three of us, each leaning forward, notebooks in hand, eagerly waiting for some ordinary bloke, who had already put in a hard day's work and was now giving up his evening to serve the community, to utter something controversial that we could then pounce on for our respective papers, such rivalry seemed slightly ridiculous and I began to feel self-conscious about what I was doing for the first time. It was worse when several of us would turn up at a mundane event like an annual flower show or gymkhana as if it were some local sensation, and I came to dread the jostling for titbits that took place on such occasions. It was not that I feared competition – the Journal more than held its own in this respect – it was just that it seemed so absurd in a rural context. We sometimes arranged for just one of us to cover an event and supply the others with "blacks" but the Journal tended to come off worst from this arrangement because it appeared last, and it was also possible that by attending the event yourself, you could spot something interesting that the others might miss.

The Cotswold community itself was also changing. There were many, many newcomers and fewer of the old faces to be seen. I had not realised how many of the people I knew were so much older than I was, those of my own generation having left the area in pursuit of a career or a house. A disadvantage of living in the same place for a long time is that you are constantly reminded of your neighbour's, and thus your own, mortality. Most of the public figures, whom I had revered as a young man when they were in their prime, had long since been eulogised in our obituary column and none of similar stature had come along to replace them, or so it appeared to me, looking back through a veil of nostalgia.

A further turn of the screw came when a friend living in a different part of the country rang to say that a member of his family had been caught shoplifting and was to appear before the magistrates. He wanted to know whether it would be possible to ask the editor of his local paper not to report the case, the publicity being a far worse punishment than any fine the court might impose. I soon put him right about this and told him not to approach the editor or engage a solicitor if a plea of "Guilty" were proposed, but to keep the proceedings as low key and unobtrusive as possible. He kept regularly in touch with me during the weeks that followed and it became obvious that the impending case was tearing the family apart. The atmosphere at home was poisonous and all were agreed they could no longer go on living in the town, where they felt their reputation would be irreparably damaged. Consequently, they started looking at houses, which they did not want, in another town, where they did not want to live, with a view to moving away as soon as practicable. When the case came to court, it had to be postponed until after lunch because there was such a heavy agenda that morning and when the court resumed and the case was heard, none of the reporters, who had crowded the Press bench during the morning, had seen fit to return; the case went unreported, there was no unfavourable publicity, the family's secret was kept, there was no need for them to move, and they all lived happily ever after. (It is ironic that newspapers should make such an issue about hearings in private when they, themselves, condone such a practice by not bothering to send reporters to what must be hundreds of court cases every day.)

The family's anxiety had inadvertently been transferred to me. I had always thought of myself as being a harmless sort of person but now I began to wonder what effect my court reporting was having on accused people and whether their families were having to go through the same misery as my friend's had done. It could be argued that such individuals had only themselves to blame for their predicament though it could equally be said that the fine or other penalty imposed by the court was the legal punishment for their offence and that the publicity, causing them the greater anguish, was a superfluous torment. My feelings were aggravated by the fact that the magistrates were regularly dividing themselves into two courts and I was being forced more and more into choosing which cases to report and which not. If a sitting went on after lunch, the question also arose of whether to come back after the adjournment. I wanted to do so in order to treat everyone the same but my colleagues were less keen, unless it was a major case, and they would ask me to ring them with the details later, which only worsened the situation by making me the sole discloser of someone's fall from grace.

For the first time I began to think the unthinkable: of what life might be like without the Journal, and when a new publication started in my patch in 1981, not quite a newspaper and not quite a free sheet but a menace in either form, and the immediate reaction of our management was to put up the price of the Journal yet again, I came close to chucking in the job. The only reason I hesitated was that it would look as though I had been frightened away by our new opponent.

Soon afterwards Berrow's Newspapers changed hands again. This time they were sold by Mr. Murdoch, who was having to finance his purchase of The Times, to Reed International, owners of the Daily Mirror and numerous women's magazines, providing the Journal with further unlikely partners. In the past, the various changes of ownership had not affected the editorial side of the paper but this was no longer true. The new owners were prepared to spend generously in putting Berrow's into good shape but had their own ideas about what sort of papers they wanted and were not entirely pleased with those they had inherited. They had good cause for believing changes to be necessary . Several of Berrow's papers had been badly mauled by the free sheets and the Journal's sales were falling, too. It was a bitter pill when our circulation went under 20,000 for the first time.

The new management were obsessed with the free sheets though I considered that other factors were also responsible for the decline in sales, not least our frequent price rises. All the free sheets I knew looked like second-rate magazines and the obvious way to hold them, I thought, was by emphasising the difference between them and us: in other words, by contrasting their risible news coverage with the comprehensive service and professional presentation that the Journal had at its fingertips. However, the management's tactics had the effect, if anything, of making the Journal look less like a newspaper and more like a free sheet. The paper had always had too much news chasing not enough space and copy had to be spiked or held over every week of

The Giants Move In

the year. We were now told to carry more features with the result that further news had to be omitted to make room for superfluous articles and the photographers, whose black-and-white pictures were widely admired, were told to go over to the more costly colour process for their photos.

Other expenditure went on adapting a building at Worcester as a training centre for Berrow's staff, the prospect of attending which filled me with apprehension, and the production of a house journal, in colour, for free distribution within the organisation. If this publication were intended to promote goodwill, it had the opposite effect, where I was concerned. Every issue displayed a picture gallery of executives joining the firm, no doubt at salaries commensurate with their station, and as one of the hardworking Indians, I seethed at the appointment of so many new Chiefs.

When it came, my departure was easier and more lucrative than I had expected. In August of 1983, all employers of Berrow's received a confidential letter saying that despite the money spent, the future of the organisation was at risk unless drastic action were taken. Two papers were to be closed and two others sold. Another four were to be paired with the free sheets that had so debilitated them, and this was to be achieved by the formation of a joint company consisting of Berrow's and the free sheet publishers. These moves would free resources to build up the remaining newspapers, including the Journal, though some job losses would have to take place. It was hoped that the losses could be achieved by voluntary redundancy and details were given of the terms on offer to those interested in volunteering.

It was obvious that the company intended to keep the Journal going and that the offer of voluntary redundancy was aimed mainly at staff on papers to disappear or be linked to the free sheets, yet the letter was addressed to all employees and could thus be regarded as applicable to those of us on reprieved papers, too. If so, it seemed a golden opportunity to get out with some money in my pocket. Better this than to continue working for a management with whose ideas I was so out of sympathy, then quit after a year or so without a penny, and so I decided to chance my luck and put in for redundancy.

At the risk of sounding conceited, I never thought they would let me go. By this time I knew more about the North Cotswolds than any other person and had become a typical journeyman reporter doing everything that came my way and doing it fast, not to mention taking and writing advertising copy: the sort of employee you would have thought a management would bind unto itself with bands of steel. But they did! The applications from my colleagues at Tewkesbury and Stratford were also accepted, leaving no-one outside Evesham, and possibly disheartened by this prospect, the Editor also decided to go. I can only suppose that the links between management and the grass roots had, indeed, become so tenuous that they were unaware of our usefulness. It was the sort of situation to be expected where all that a far-off proprietor knows of his newspaper is whether it is in the black or not. Within three months of my departure, the office in Moreton High Street, the Journal's shop window in the Cotswolds, had been sold and converted into a dress shop and the area covered by a reporter based at Evesham. It was almost as though the previous 40 years had never existed.

My relief at going was marred with regret that the reporting link between the Cotswold council at Cirencester and the North Cotswolds would be weakened, if not broken, and that the people of the district would not longer be receiving information they were entitled to have. On the other hand, with a news editor giving us our daily instructions, it was by no means certain that I would be allowed to continue going to Cirencester anyway.

A deeper and more painful cause for regret came with the realisation that leaving the Journal meant that I would also have to leave the Cotswolds. By approving my redundancy, the firm had caught me on the hop. I lived in "tied" accommodation over the office and had neither the time nor the cash to buy somewhere else; or to be more precise, I had the money but if I spent it all on property, I would be obliged to find another job at once to support me, and this was something that could not be taken for granted at my age and with my limited work experience. I had fallen into the old Cotswold trap of high-priced housing on one hand and lack of employment opportunity on the other that had driven many a Cotswoldian out of the area before me, and when offered the top floor of a relative's large house in the county of Avon, I accepted it as the only immediate solution to my problems, and prepared to bid farewell to the hills that had been my workshop for so long.

Needless to say, the Cotswolds had changed greatly during the forty years that I had travelled them by bicycle, motorcycle and car as a district reporter, and not all the changes had been for the better. Although the standard of living had improved along with that of the

The Giants Move In

rest of the country, the quality of life had diminished in many ways due to those two bugbears of the age, the internal combustion engine and centralisation. All the Cotswold towns and villages had lost something in one way or another. Blockley, Campden, Stow and Bourton-on-the-Water had lost their railway stations; Moreton, its magistrates' court and employment exchange, and Stow, its county court. The gas works had gone from Moreton, Campden, Bourton and Stow. Many villages, such as Evenlode, Todenham, and Bourton-on-the-Hill, had lost their schools and others, like the Guitings, Slaughters, Oddington and Adlestrop no longer had their own village parson but shared him with other parishes, often as many as five or six together. The majority of the changes had their roots in improved private transport. It was easier for people to get about now that they had their own cars. The transfer of the district council from Moreton to Cirencester would have been impossible had not the use of the private car become so widespread. Children could be taken to a centralised school by bus. Parsons and their congregations could move from church to church for their services. Stations must close because people preferred to use their cars instead of the trains. Worse still, rural bus services disappeared through lack of passengers. It was a hard life in the remoter Cotswolds if you did not have a car.

All the small towns had succumbed to tourist traffic, which did not just mean congested streets and parking problems. It also meant more and bigger traffic signs, ice cream vans, hot dog stalls and litter. At Bourton, Stow and even pretty little Lower Slaughter it had also meant being showered with yellow lines. The odd thing was that this influx of traffic had not given a noticeable boost to trade. Both Campden and Blockley had lost a number of important shops; Moreton had lost a department store but, like Stow, had gained a large number of antique shops.

Apart from the fact that more people had cars, televisions and refrigerators, the most obvious gain was that the appearance of the district had been greatly improved as a result of old houses and cottages being modernised and derelict farm buildings converted into attractive homes. Some villages, like Guiting Power, Evenlode and Broadwell, had been transformed almost out of recognition. There was a greater awareness everywhere of conservation, tidiness and the importance of planning, the latter subject generating more argument in town and village than any other.

The big problem was still housing. Much private building had gone into putting up expensive homes not for local people but for the well-to-do retired from outside the district. In places like Campden it had become impossible for a young couple to buy a cheap house, and it was particularly galling for them and others similarly placed throughout the district to see mini-mansions going up which were beyond their financial reach and which tended to result in the average age of the district being forced up another notch. Parish councils were no help. They begged for cheaper houses but when such a scheme was presented to them, rejected it because of "high density". Fortunately, the Cotswold District Council were more broadminded, remembering, perhaps, that these historic conservation areas, which they had been designating in Cotswold towns and villages, had a far higher "density" than any modern scheme was likely to have. The great challenge for the future was undoubtedly cheaper houses in the Cotswolds or more houses to rent, which, if met, would keep younger people with families in the district even though it would be too late to save an old timer like me from having to emigrate. My exile was to last two years.

Some things never seemed to change, however. The major story of my last weeks with the Journal was the flooding of Campden on two occasions within almost a month of each other, both calamities caused, so the experts opined, by the kind of freak rainstorm experienced only once in a hundred years. Some wags said the first storm must have been at the end of the first hundred years and the second, at the beginning of the second hundred! It all reminded me of a ballad I had written nearly thirty years before about previous Campden floods, which no-one wanted to put right for fear of having to foot the bill, using the complexities of the drainage laws as an excuse for inaction. Let this sad song be my valedictory!

Oh, Mary put the boards up!
It's raining hard tonight!
The water's all around us,
It is a fearful sight!
So board you up the front door
And I'll board up the back.
The floods are rising fast, love,
Alas and alack!

We asked the Parish Council
To drive the floods away;

The Giants Move In

They said, "We'd like to help you
But who is going to pay?"
The water's round my ankles:
It's pouring through the door.
Oh, Mary, see the carpets
Afloat on the floor!

We asked the District Council
To remedy our plight:
They said, "We have no power,
The Drainage Acts aren't right."
And now, my love, the water
Is splashing round my knees.
Will no-one in the wide world
Give ear to our pleas?

We tried the County Council:
They said, "We cannot spend
Our money to stop flooding
When we have roads to mend."
The tide has reached my waistline,
Its grip is sharp and chill.
Ere dawn we shall have tasted
Of water our fill!

The Minister of Housing
Was begged to save our souls:
He said, "I'm quite bewildered,
The Law's so full of holes."
So here we are a-standing
In water shoulder high
While furniture and sprout stalks
Float silently by!

There's no one left to help us!
Alas! Our fate is sealed!
The floods cannot be halted
For laws to be repealed.
The water's round my neck now:
It's spinning like a hub!
Oh, Mary dear, I'm drownded!
I'm… glub-uggle-glub.

INDEX

Abbotswood House 82
Adlestrop 150
Alcester 9, 11
American Servicemen 6, 16, 23; tourists 126
Anne, Princess 59-60
Armstrong-Jones, Anthony (later Lord Snowdon) 30
Askwith, Robin, actor 91
Aston Subedge 64-66
Attlee, Clement (Prime Minister 1945-51) 29
Avon, River 1, 6

Baldwin, George 116
Ballard, George scholar 85
Banbury Guardian 144
Bangalore, India 71
Barbirolli, Sir John 134
Barton-on-the-Heath 52, 101
Bathurst, Earl 114
Batsford Park 4, 32, 59, 82
Belas Knap, burial mound 4
Benfield, Fred 50
Benfield, Tom 42
Benson, Lady Violet 82
Berrows Newspapers 14, 116-122, 143-4, 147-9
Bidford-on-Avon 72
Birmingham 9, 23, 38
Birmingham Post 108-10
Bledisloe Cup 114-5
Blockley 18; character of 33-5; silk mills 33, old trout 33-4;
   suicides 35; electric light 35; flower show 37; parish council 96, 98, 150
Bough, Emily 77-8
Bourne, John, farmer 26
Bourton-on-the-Hill 22, 150
Bourton-on-the-Water 18, 23-4; character of 35-7; tourism 35-7; model
   village 35-6; brass bands 37; flower show 37; amateur drama 89-90;
   parish council 96, 98; 150
Bredon Hill 1, 4, 51
B.B.C. 65, 105
Broadway tower 1, 124; Lygon Arms 29
Broadwell 23, 150
Brodie, Les, mayor 39
Broom 72, 74
Browning, Frank, reporter 133-5
Buckland, Ernie 39
Burden, George, council clerk 41-2
Burns, Dr. Francis 52
Burnt Norton House 83-6

Carr family, newspaper owners 143
Capers, William, centenarian 64-6
Centenarians 63-6
Central Flying School 59
Charlecote House 4
Charles, Prince of Wales 59-61
Chastleton House 4
Cheltenham district council 130, 133-5
Chipping Campden 10-11, 17-8, 22; political meetings 26-28; character of 37-40; newcomers 37-40; street lighting 38-9; wishing well 39-40; Women's Institute tree 50; Royal British Legion 50; parish council 96, 98; school play 103-4; 141-2, 150-1; flooding 151-2
Chipping Norton 4, 108-10
Cirencester 130-3
Civil Defence 23
Clarke, Bill, reporter 111
Clifton, Gerald, butcher 107
Coalmining 17-8
Compton Wynyates House 4
Conscription 3, 16-7
Conservative Party 27-9
Coronation of Elizabeth II 49-50
Coroner's Court 80-1
Cotswold District Council 60-1, 130-2, 149-51
Cotswold pennycress 47-8
Cotswold Way 126
Coughton Court 4
Cresswell, Major Estcourt 84
Crook, Fred, reporter 10
Cutsdean 130

Daily Telegraph 106
Davies, Tony, council clerk 37
Day, Barry, author's father 1-3, 17, 99, 108, 113
Day, David vi; leaves school 1-3; joins Evesham Journal 3-6, 7-10, 13-14; war years 6-7, 12-3, 16-7; appointed to Moreton-in-Marsh 18-20; motor cycling 20-1; post-war austerity 21-2; district reporting 25-6; political coverage 26-30; links with head office 44; stays with the Harveys 44-6; relations with farmers 46-8; visiting London 48-9; work routines 53-5; encounters with royalty 58-62; interviews with centenarians 63-6; wedding anniversaries 66-8; Shakespeare stories 69-74; court reporting 76-7; 79-80; reviewing plays 87-90; play acting 90-3; covering parish councils 95-8; selling copy 105-7; Rollright Stones blunder 107-10; buys car 112-3; father's death 113; joins National Union of Journalists 117-9; moves into Fielding House 119-20; producing front-page news 121-2; cross country walking 127-9; covers Cotswold District Council 131-2; experiences with Cheltenham District Council 133-4; vehicle breakdowns 137-42; change of employers 143-4, 147; offset problems 144; disenchantment with job 145-7; leaves Cotswolds 148-9

Daylesford House 82
Dee, Charlie, farmer 83
Deerhurst 4
Dickenson, Bob, newsvendor 59
Displaced Persons 22
Donovan, Councillor Amy 37
Dover's Games Society 39-40, 50-3
Drayton, Michael, poet 50
Duckworth, Leslie, news editor 108-10
Dugdale family 59
Dulverton, 1st Baron 32, 82

Edgehill, Battle of 4
Edinburgh, Duke of 59
Edward VII 59
Edwards, Bill, farmer 55-6
Eliot, Thomas Stearns, poet 84
Elizabeth II 22, 49-50, 111
Elizabeth, Queen Mother 59
Ellis, Mike, reporter 44
Evenlode 55-6, 66-7, 100, 123, 150
Everyman Theatre, Cheltenham 87, 137-8
Evesham 1-2, 4-5, 9, 18-9, 22, 44, 51, 83, 104, 108, 124
Evesham Journal 2-4, 7-9, 13; Moreton-in-Marsh office 18-20, 44, 53; centenary of 111-2; ownership changes 116-7, 143-4
Evesham Standard 14, 116
Exhall 72-4

Farming 46-7
Ferguson, Harry, tractor magnate 82
Festival of Britain 49-50
Fire Service Training College 59
Fladbury 16
Fleet Street 29-30, 60; linage 105-7
Flying Saucers 55-6
Food Control Committee 22
Ford hamlet 130
Ford, Henry, auto millionaire 101
Fosse Way 24, 31, 40, 128, 131-2
Four Shires Stone 31
Fowler, Ron 116
Free sheets 144-5, 147-8
Fuel Economy Committee 22
Funerals 99-100

Galloway, Councillor Norman 37
Galt, John, farmer 83
Garne, William, sheep farmer 48
George VI 50, 59

Gloucestershire 3, 130; county council 130
Gloucestershire Echo 60, 132-3
Godman, Lieut-col John 77-8
Golden weddings 11-2, 66-8
Gooding, Harry, slater 101
Grace, Dr W.G. 32
Grafton 72-3
Grant-Adamson, David, reporter 44
Grevel, William, wool merchant 11
Guiting Power 63-4, 126, 130, 150

Hailes Abbey 4
Halle Orchestra 134
Hamilton, Judge Alistor 76
Harris, Denzil 116
Harrowby, Earl of, see Sandon
Harveys, Bill and Norris 44-6, 53, 120
Hathaway, Anne 73
Haynes, Bill, farmer 86
Hidcote Manor Gardens 101-3
Hill, James, solicitor 75
Hillborough 73
Hoare family 108-10
Home Guard 7
Honeybourne 16, 61
Hopla, Ken 116
Horne, Jim 116
Housing 46, 113, 115-6, 150-1
Hudson, Beatrice 22

Improvement grants 113, 115-6
Ismay, General Lord 49

James brothers, Sam and John 101
Johnston, Major Lawrence 101-3
Jones, Alan, headmaster 104
Journalists, National Union of 117-9; training scheme 135-7

Kemerton 104
Kennedy, President John 103-4
Keyte, Sir William 84-5
Kineton Thorns 47-8
Kleinwort, Sir Cyril, banker 82
Knee Brook 123-4

Labour Party 27, 107
Ladbrook, Bert , farmer 85-6
Laughton, Charles, actor 71
Lenches, the 5

Linage 105-110
Lloyds, Percy and Gwen 19, 49
Long Marston 72-3
Lower Slaughter 115, 130, 150
Lower Swell 130

Macmillan, Harold, Minister of Housing (later Prime Minister) 29
Magistrates' courts 10-11, 22, 61, 75-9, 112-3, 146-7, 150
Malvern Hills 4, 51
Margaret, Princess 30
Mary, Queen, widow of George V 59, 61-2
Mickleton 61-2, 102
Ministry of Fuel and Power 22
Mitford family 32, 59
Monnington, Reginald, editor 2-3, 13-14, 17, 111
Montgomery, Field Marshal Sir Bernard 71
Moreton-in-Marsh 18-20, 25-6, 28-9; character of 31-3; duck pond 53-55; royal visits 58-9; parish council 96-8; R.A.F. Station 107; effects of National Service 116; 131, 149-50
Morgan, Bob 116
Morris, "Bo", hotelier 35
Motor cycling 20-1, 44
Moulson, Mickey 116
Murdoch, Rupert, newspaper mogul 143, 147

Nabarro, Gerald, M.P. 29-30
National Farmers' Union 5, 29-30, 47, 106-7, 117
National Gallery 83
National Service 116
Naunton 130
Nelson, Jack 39-40
Newbould, Les 116
News International 143
News Of The World 143
Newspaper Society 58
New Zealand 107
Nobes, Frank 39
Noel, Penelope, her monument 11
North Cotswold District Council 18, 129-30
Northleach 24, 126, 128-9; district council 130
Northwick park camp 22; mansion 82-3, 86

Oddington 150
Offset printing 144-5
Oil drilling 126
Organ, Bill, farmer 85
Oxfordshire 4, 23, 31
Oxpens hamlet 129
Oxford Times 144

Parish councils 94-8
Pasolini, Pier Paolo, film director 90-2
Pasque flower 47-8
Pearce, Edward, gardener 101-3
Pebworth 71, 73
Pershore 3-4, 10, 44, 124
Phillips, Les, reporter 14-7
Phillips, Hon Wogan (later Lord Milford) 28-9
Playhouse cinema 56-7, 92-3
Police 25, 53, 79-81
Political coverage 26-30
Prew, Ernest and Priscilla 67-8
Price, Police superintendent E.J. 10
Prisoners-of-war 21, 57

Ragley Hall 4
Railway (Paddington–Worcester) 18, 31-2, 48, 115, 122-5
Red Arrows aerobatic team 59
Redesdale Hall 32, 54
Reed International 147-8
Rissington Mill 127
Rollright Stones 4, 107-10
Rothermere, Lord 82
Royal Shakespeare Theatre 69-71, 87, 104
Royal visits 58-62

Sanders, Peter, solicitor 78-9
Sandon, Viscount (later Earl of Harrowby) 83-6
Sartre, Jean-Paul, playwright 89-90
Saunders, Henry, solicitor 10
School Certificate 1-3
Severn, River 4, 23, 124
Sezincote House 4, 82
Shakespeare, William, poet 4, 50, 52, 69-74
Shipston-on-Stour 124
Simpson, Eric, reporter 44
Smith family, newspaper owners 7-9, 111-2
Spencer-Churchill, Captain George 82-3
Springhill estate 67; prisoner-of-war camp 22
Stanley, Wally 38
Stanway House 4, 82
Steele, George, farmer 47
Steward, Councillor Joe 37
Stewart, Seumas 40, 52
Stow-on-the-Wold 4, 18, 24; character of 40-3; swillies 42-3;
    courthouse 75-81; parish council 96, 98, 113; royal visit 60;
    gasworks 75-6; amateur drama 88-9; 150
Stratford-upon-Avon 4; branch office 9, 44, 121, 149; 65;
    tourist attraction 69-70; 104, 116, 124

159

Stretton-on-Fosse 103
Stribbling, Gerry, reporter 60
Sudeley Castle 4, 29
Sun, daily newspaper 143
Swan Theatre, Worcester 87
Swindon Evening Advertiser 60, 132

Tarplett, David 116
Taylor, Councillor John 37
Television 49, 56
Temple Guiting 130, 150
Tetbury District Council 130
Tewkesbury 4, 44; branch office 121, 133, 149, 124, 130, 139
Thomas, George, cinema owner 56-7
Times, newspaper 54, 106, 144, 147
Todenham 150
Udale, Ann, centenarian 63-4
Upper Slaughter 115, 130, 150
Upper Swell 130
Upton, Ken, photographer 92

Vincent, Martin, reporter 60

Walker brothers, Roy and Derek 116
War, Second World 3, 6-7; casualties 12-3; author's call-up 16-7; D-Day landings 16
Warwickshire 3, 31, 130
Wasson, Danny 28-9
Way, Rev. Hilary 41
Weaver, Sam, farmer 66-7
Wedding anniversaries 66-8
Whateley, Anne 73
Whitehouse, Derrick 116
Wilts. and Glos. Standard 132, 144
Winchcombe 4
Windrush, River 35
Wixford 12, 72-3
Women's Land Army 61-2
Wool trade 24
Woolley, Councillor Ben 37
Worcestershire 3, 31

Young Farmers' Club 88

Z-Reservists 107